# Introduction to *Daily Paragraph Editing*

## Why *Daily Paragraph Editing?*

*Daily Paragraph Editing* is designed to help students master and retain grade-level skills in language mechanics and expression through focused, daily practice. Instead of practicing skills in a series of random, decontextualized exercises, *Daily Paragraph Editing* embeds language skills in paragraphs that represent the types of text that students encounter in their daily reading and writing activities across the curriculum. A weekly writing activity allows students to apply the skills they have been practicing throughout the week in their own short compositions.

## What's in *Daily Paragraph Editing?*

*Daily Paragraph Editing* contains lessons for 36 weeks, with a separate lesson for each day.

Each week's lessons for Monday through Thursday consist of individual reproducible paragraphs that contain errors in the following skills:

- capitalization
- punctuation
- spelling
- language usage, and more

## Student's daily lesson pages for Monday through Thursday include:

- a label indicating the type of writing modeled in the weekly lesson

- a paragraph with errors for students to correct; along with the other 3 paragraphs for the week, this forms a complete composition

- daily and weekly lesson identifiers

- as needed, the "Watch For" logo alerts students to more challenging skills to address in the paragraph

BIOGRAPHY: Jane Goodall: Learning About Animals

Daily Paragraph Editing

Name _____

### Jane Goodall: Learning About Animals

what would your mother say if you took worms to bed. what if you hid in a chicken hous for hours. a little girl growing up in england did these things Her name was jane Goodall

WATCH FOR

- names of people and places
- question marks

MONDAY

WEEK 1

Students correct the errors in each daily paragraph by marking directly on the page. A reproducible sheet of Proofreading Marks (see page 10) helps familiarize students with the standard form for marking corrections on written text. Full-page Editing Keys show corrections for all errors in the daily paragraphs. Error Summaries help teachers identify the targeted skills in each week's lessons, and therefore help teachers plan to review or introduce the specific skills needed by their students.

**Teacher's full-sized annotated Editing Key pages include:**

• a label indicating the type of writing modeled in the weekly lesson

• the original student text with corrections marked in red (using the proofreading marks presented on page 10)

• daily and weekly lesson identifiers

• a summary of the errors in each paragraph to use in identifying unfamiliar skills to teach or review with students prior to assigning the paragraph. Some students may be more successful if you share the Error Summary with them before they read and edit the paragraph.

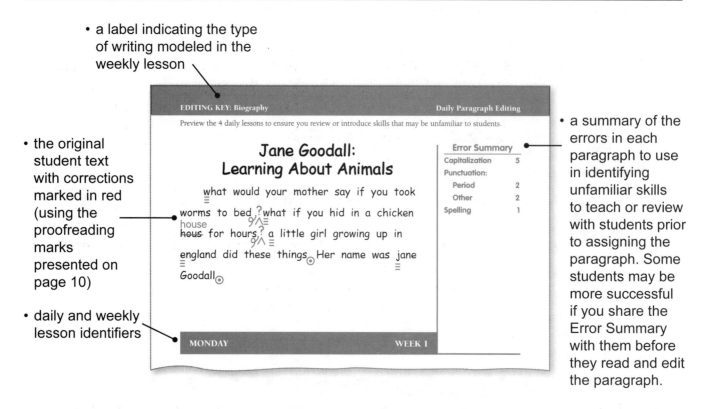

When corrected and read together, the four paragraphs for one week's lesson form a cohesive composition that also serves as a writing model for students. The weekly four-paragraph compositions cover a broad range of expository and narrative writing forms from across the curriculum, including the following:

• nonfiction texts on grade-level topics in social studies and science
• biographies, book reviews, editorials, instructions, interviews, journal entries, and letters
• fables, fantasy and science fiction, historical fiction, personal narratives, and realistic fiction

Each Friday lesson consists of a writing prompt that directs students to write in response to the week's four-paragraph composition. This gives students the opportunity to apply the skills they have practiced during the week in their own writing. Students gain experience writing in a wide variety of forms, always with the support of familiar models.

## Friday writing prompts include:

- a prompt to write a composition in the same form as modeled in the weekly lesson

- sample topic sentences to support reluctant writers

- a weekly lesson identifier

- hints to help students address skills that are specific to the writing form

- a label indicating the type of writing modeled in the weekly lesson

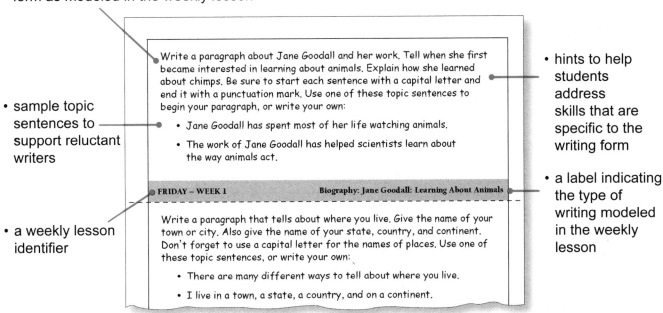

Write a paragraph about Jane Goodall and her work. Tell when she first became interested in learning about animals. Explain how she learned about chimps. Be sure to start each sentence with a capital letter and end it with a punctuation mark. Use one of these topic sentences to begin your paragraph, or write your own:

- Jane Goodall has spent most of her life watching animals.
- The work of Jane Goodall has helped scientists learn about the way animals act.

FRIDAY – WEEK 1                 Biography: Jane Goodall: Learning About Animals

Write a paragraph that tells about where you live. Give the name of your town or city. Also give the name of your state, country, and continent. Don't forget to use a capital letter for the names of places. Use one of these topic sentences, or write your own:

- There are many different ways to tell about where you live.
- I live in a town, a state, a country, and on a continent.

An Editing Checklist for students (see page 11) helps them revise their own writing or critique their peers' efforts. An Assessment Rubric (see page 9) is provided to help you assess student writing.

A reproducible student Language Handbook (pages 168–176) outlines the usage and mechanics rules for students to follow in editing the daily paragraphs. The Handbook includes examples to help familiarize students with how the conventions of language and mechanics are applied in authentic writing.

# How to Use *Daily Paragraph Editing*

You may use *Daily Paragraph Editing* in several ways, depending on your instructional objectives and your students' needs. Over time, you will probably want to introduce each of the presentation strategies outlined below so you can identify the approach that works best for you and your students.

The four paragraphs that comprise each week's editing lessons include a set of errors that are repeated throughout all four paragraphs. We recommend that you provide a folder for students to keep their *Daily Paragraph Editing* reference materials and weekly lessons. It will work best to reproduce and distribute all four daily paragraphs for a given week on Monday. That way, students can use the previous days' lessons for reference as the week progresses.

## Directed Group Lessons

*Daily Paragraph Editing* activities will be most successful if you first introduce them as a group activity. You might also have students edit individual copies of the day's lesson as you work through the paragraph with the group. Continue presenting the Monday through Thursday lessons to the entire class until you are confident that students are familiar with the editing process. Try any of the following methods to direct group lessons:

### Option 1

1. Create and display an overhead transparency of the day's paragraph.

2. Read the paragraph aloud just as it is written, including all the errors.

3. Read the paragraph a second time, using phrasing and intonation that would be appropriate if all end punctuation were correct. (You may find it helpful to read from the Editing Key.) Read all other errors as they appear in the text.

4. Guide students in correcting all end punctuation and initial capitals in the paragraph; mark corrections in erasable pen on the overhead transparency.

5. After the paragraph is correctly divided into sentences, review it one sentence at a time. Have volunteers point out errors as you come to them, and identify the necessary corrections. Encourage students to explain the reason for each correction; explain or clarify any rules that are unfamiliar.

EMC 2725 • Daily Paragraph Editing • ©2004 by Evan-Moor Corp.

## Option 2

Follow Steps 1–4 on page 4, and then work with students to focus on one type of error at a time, correcting all errors of the same type (i.e., capitalization, commas, subject/verb agreement, spelling, etc.) in the paragraph before moving on to another type. Refer to the Error Summary in the Editing Key to help you identify the various types of errors.

## Option 3

Use directed group lesson time to conduct a minilesson on one or more of the skills emphasized in that day's lesson. This is especially appropriate for new or unfamiliar skills, or for skills that are especially challenging or confusing for students. After introducing a specific skill, use the approach outlined in Option 2 to focus on that skill in one or more of the week's daily paragraphs. To provide additional practice, refer to the Skills Scope & Sequence to find other paragraphs that include the same target skill.

## Individual Practice

Once students are familiar with the process for editing the daily paragraphs, they may work on their own or with a partner to make corrections. Be sure students have their Proofreading Marks (see page 10) available to help them mark their corrections. Remind students to refer to the student Language Handbook as needed for guidance in the rules of mechanics and usage. Some students may find it helpful to know at the outset the number and types of errors they are seeking. Provide this information by referring to the Error Summary on the annotated Editing Key pages. You may wish to use a transparency on the overhead to check work with the group. Occasionally, you may wish to assess students' acquisition of skills by collecting and reviewing their work before they check it.

## Customizing Instruction

Some of the skills covered in *Daily Paragraph Editing* may not be part of the grade-level expectancies in the language program you use. Some skills may even be taught differently in your program from the way they are modeled in *Daily Paragraph Editing*. In such cases, follow the approach used in your program. Simply revise the paragraph text as needed by covering it with correction fluid or by writing in changes before you reproduce copies for students.

Comma usage is an area where discrepancies are most likely to arise. *Daily Paragraph Editing* uses the "closed" style, where commas are included after short introductory phrases. Except for commas used in salutations, closings, dates, and between city and state in letters, journals, or news articles, all commas that appear in the daily paragraphs have been correctly placed according to the closed style. All other skills related to the use of commas are practiced by requiring students to insert missing commas, rather than moving or deleting extraneous commas.

Occasionally, you or your students may make a correction that differs from that shown in the Editing Key. The decision to use an exclamation mark instead of a period, or a period instead of a semicolon, is often a subjective decision made by individual writers. When discrepancies of this sort arise, capitalize on the "teachable moment" to let students know that there are gray areas in English usage and mechanics, and discuss how each of the possible correct choices can affect the meaning or tone of the writing.

You may wish to have your students mark corrections on the daily paragraphs in a manner that differs from the common proofreading marks on page 10. If so, model the marking style you wish students to follow as you conduct group lessons on an overhead, and point out any differences between the standard proofing marks and those to be used by your students.

## Using the Writing Prompts

Have students keep their daily paragraphs in a folder so they can review the week's four corrected paragraphs on Friday. Identify the type of writing modeled in the four-paragraph composition and any of its special features (e.g., dialog in a fictional narrative; salutation, closing, and paragraph style in a letter; opinion statements and supporting arguments in an editorial; etc.).

Present the Friday writing prompt on an overhead transparency, write it on the board, or distribute individual copies to students. Take a few minutes to brainstorm ideas with the group and to focus on language skills that students will need to address in their writing.

After students complete their writing, encourage them to use the Editing Checklist to review or revise their work. You may also wish to have partners review each other's writing. To conduct a more formal assessment of students' writing, use the Assessment Rubric on page 9.

If you assign paragraph writing for homework, be sure students have the week's four corrected paragraphs available as a reference. You may wish to set aside some time for volunteers to read their completed writing to the class, or display compositions on a weekly writing bulletin board for students to enjoy.

# Skills Scope and Sequence

**Week No.**

## Capitalization

| Skill | 1 | 2 | 3 | 4 | 5 | 6 | 7 | 8 | 9 | 10 | 11 | 12 | 13 | 14 | 15 | 16 | 17 | 18 | 19 | 20 | 21 | 22 | 23 | 24 | 25 | 26 | 27 | 28 | 29 | 30 | 31 | 32 | 33 | 34 | 35 | 36 |
|---|---|---|---|---|---|---|---|---|---|---|---|---|---|---|---|---|---|---|---|---|---|---|---|---|---|---|---|---|---|---|---|---|---|---|---|---|
| Beginning of Sentences, Quotations, Salutations/Closings | • | | • | • | • | • | | • | | • | | | | • | • | • | | | • | • | • | • | • | • | • | • | • | • | • | • | • | • | • | • | • | • |
| Days & Months | | | | • | | • | | | | | | | • | • | | | | • | • | | | | | | | | • | | • | | • | | | | | |
| Holidays | | | | | | | | | | | | • | • | • | | | • | | | | | | | | | | • | | | | | | | | | |
| Incorrect Use of Capitals | | | | | | | • | • | • | | • | | | | • | | • | • | | | | | • | | | | | • | • | | | | • | | | |
| Names & Titles of People, Nationalities | • | | • | | • | | | | | | | • | | • | • | | | | | | | | • | | • | | • | • | • | • | | • | • | • | • | • |
| Names of Places | • | | | | | • | | • | | | | | | | | | | | | | | • | • | • | | | • | • | • | | | • | | • | | |
| Nouns Used as Names (Aunt, Grandpa, etc.) | | | | | | | | | | | | • | • | | | | | | | | | | | | | | | | | | | | | | | |
| Titles of Books, Magazines, Poems, Stories | | | | | | | | | | | • | | | | | • | | | | | | | | | • | | • | | | | | | • | | | |
| Word I | | | | • | | | | | | | • | | | • | | | | | | | | | | | • | | | | | | | | | | • | |

## Language Usage

| Skill | 1 | 2 | 3 | 4 | 5 | 6 | 7 | 8 | 9 | 10 | 11 | 12 | 13 | 14 | 15 | 16 | 17 | 18 | 19 | 20 | 21 | 22 | 23 | 24 | 25 | 26 | 27 | 28 | 29 | 30 | 31 | 32 | 33 | 34 | 35 | 36 |
|---|---|---|---|---|---|---|---|---|---|---|---|---|---|---|---|---|---|---|---|---|---|---|---|---|---|---|---|---|---|---|---|---|---|---|---|---|
| Correct Use of Singular & Plural Forms | | | | | • | | | | • | | • | | | | | | | | | • | | | • | | | | | | | • | | | | | | |
| Correct Use of Verb Tenses | | | | | | | | | | | | | | | | | | | | • | | | | | | | | | | | | | • | | | |
| Use of Correct Adjective & Adverbial Forms | | | • | | • | | | | | | | | | | | | | | | | | | | | | | | | | | | | | | • | |
| Use of Correct Pronouns | | | • | | | | | | | | | | | | | | | | | • | | | | | | | | | | | | | | | | |

## Punctuation: Apostrophes

| Skill | 1 | 2 | 3 | 4 | 5 | 6 | 7 | 8 | 9 | 10 | 11 | 12 | 13 | 14 | 15 | 16 | 17 | 18 | 19 | 20 | 21 | 22 | 23 | 24 | 25 | 26 | 27 | 28 | 29 | 30 | 31 | 32 | 33 | 34 | 35 | 36 |
|---|---|---|---|---|---|---|---|---|---|---|---|---|---|---|---|---|---|---|---|---|---|---|---|---|---|---|---|---|---|---|---|---|---|---|---|---|
| In Contractions | | | | • | • | • | | • | | | • | • | • | | • | | | | • | | • | • | | • | • | • | • | | • | • | • | • | • | • | • | • |
| In Possessives | | | • | | | | • | | | | • | | • | | | • | | | | | • | | • | • | | | | | • | | • | | • | | | |
| Improperly Placed | | | | | | | | | | | • | | | | | | | | | | | | | | | | | | | | | | | | | |

## Punctuation: Commas

| Skill | 1 | 2 | 3 | 4 | 5 | 6 | 7 | 8 | 9 | 10 | 11 | 12 | 13 | 14 | 15 | 16 | 17 | 18 | 19 | 20 | 21 | 22 | 23 | 24 | 25 | 26 | 27 | 28 | 29 | 30 | 31 | 32 | 33 | 34 | 35 | 36 |
|---|---|---|---|---|---|---|---|---|---|---|---|---|---|---|---|---|---|---|---|---|---|---|---|---|---|---|---|---|---|---|---|---|---|---|---|---|
| After Salutation & Closing in a Letter | | | | | | | | | | | | | | | | | | | • | | | | | | | • | | • | | | | | • | | | |
| Between City & State & City & Country Names | | | | | | | | | | | | | | • | | | | | | | | | | | | | | • | | | | | | | | |
| Between Items in a Series | | | • | | | • | | • | | | | | | | | | • | • | | | | • | | | | | | • | • | | | • | | | | |
| In a Date | | | • | | | | | | • | | | | | | | | | | | | | | • | | | | | | • | | • | | | • | | |
| To Set Off Quotations | | | | | | | | | | | | | | | | | | | | | | | | | | | | | | | | | • | | | |

# Skills Scope and Sequence (continued)

**Week No.**

## Punctuation: Periods

| Skill | 1 | 2 | 3 | 4 | 5 | 6 | 7 | 8 | 9 | 10 | 11 | 12 | 13 | 14 | 15 | 16 | 17 | 18 | 19 | 20 | 21 | 22 | 23 | 24 | 25 | 26 | 27 | 28 | 29 | 30 | 31 | 32 | 33 | 34 | 35 | 36 |
|---|---|---|---|---|---|---|---|---|---|---|---|---|---|---|---|---|---|---|---|---|---|---|---|---|---|---|---|---|---|---|---|---|---|---|---|---|
| At End of Sentence | • | • | • | • | • | • | • | • | • | • | • | • | • | • | • | • | • | • | • | • | • | • | • | • | • | • | • | • | • | • | • | • | • | • | • | • |
| In Time & Measurement Abbreviations | | | | • | | • | | | • | | | | | • | | | | • | | • | | • | | • | | | | | • | | | | • | | • | • |
| In Title Abbreviations | | | | | | | | | | | | • | | • | | • | | | | • | | • | • | | | | | | • | | | | | • | | • |
| In Run-on & Rambling Sentences; Fragments | • | | | | | • | • | | • | | | | | | • | | • | • | | | | | | | | • | | | | | | | | | | |

## Punctuation: Quotation Marks

| Skill | 1 | 2 | 3 | 4 | 5 | 6 | 7 | 8 | 9 | 10 | 11 | 12 | 13 | 14 | 15 | 16 | 17 | 18 | 19 | 20 | 21 | 22 | 23 | 24 | 25 | 26 | 27 | 28 | 29 | 30 | 31 | 32 | 33 | 34 | 35 | 36 |
|---|---|---|---|---|---|---|---|---|---|---|---|---|---|---|---|---|---|---|---|---|---|---|---|---|---|---|---|---|---|---|---|---|---|---|---|---|
| In Speech | • | | | | | | | • | | | | | | | • | | | | | | • | | • | • | | | • | | • | | | | • | • | • | • |
| With Titles of Poems, Short Stories, Songs | | | | | | | | | | | | • | | | | | | | | | | | | | | | | | | | | | | | | |
| Improper Placement | | | | | | | | | | | | | | | • | | | | | | | | | | | | | | | | | | | | | |

## Punctuation: Other

| Skill | 1 | 2 | 3 | 4 | 5 | 6 | 7 | 8 | 9 | 10 | 11 | 12 | 13 | 14 | 15 | 16 | 17 | 18 | 19 | 20 | 21 | 22 | 23 | 24 | 25 | 26 | 27 | 28 | 29 | 30 | 31 | 32 | 33 | 34 | 35 | 36 |
|---|---|---|---|---|---|---|---|---|---|---|---|---|---|---|---|---|---|---|---|---|---|---|---|---|---|---|---|---|---|---|---|---|---|---|---|---|
| Colon in Time | | | | | | | | | • | | | | • | | | | | • | | | | | | • | | | | | | | | | | | • | |
| Exclamation Point | | | | • | | | | | | | | • | | | | | | | | | | • | | • | | | | | | | | | | | | |
| Periods & Commas Inside Quotation Marks | | | | | | | | | | | | | | | | | | | | | | | | | | • | | | | | | | • | | • | |
| Question Mark | • | • | | | | • | | • | | | | | | • | | | | | | | • | | | • | | | • | | | • | | • | • | | | |
| Underline Titles of Books, Magazines | | | | | | | | | | | | • | | • | | | | | • | | | | | | | | • | | • | | • | | | | | |

## Spelling

| Skill | 1 | 2 | 3 | 4 | 5 | 6 | 7 | 8 | 9 | 10 | 11 | 12 | 13 | 14 | 15 | 16 | 17 | 18 | 19 | 20 | 21 | 22 | 23 | 24 | 25 | 26 | 27 | 28 | 29 | 30 | 31 | 32 | 33 | 34 | 35 | 36 |
|---|---|---|---|---|---|---|---|---|---|---|---|---|---|---|---|---|---|---|---|---|---|---|---|---|---|---|---|---|---|---|---|---|---|---|---|---|
| Identify Errors in Grade-Level Words | • | • | • | • | • | • | • | • | • | • | • | • | • | • | • | • | • | • | • | • | • | • | • | • | • | • | • | • | • | • | • | • | • | • | • | • |

EMC 2725 • Daily Paragraph Editing • ©2004 by Evan-Moor Corp.

## Assessment Rubric for Evaluating Friday Paragraph Writing

The Friday writing prompts give students the opportunity to use the capitalization, punctuation, and other usage and mechanics skills that have been practiced during the week's editing tasks. They also require students to write in a variety of different forms and genres.

In evaluating students' Friday paragraphs, you may wish to focus exclusively on their mastery of the aspects of mechanics and usage targeted that week. However, if you wish to conduct a more global assessment of student writing, the following rubric offers broad guidelines for evaluating the composition as a whole.

# Characteristics of Student Writing

| | EXCELLENT | GOOD | FAIR | WEAK |
|---|---|---|---|---|
| **Clarity and Focus** | Writing is exceptionally clear, focused, and interesting. | Writing is generally clear, focused, and interesting. | Writing is loosely focused on the topic. | Writing is unclear and unfocused. |
| **Development of Main Ideas** | Main ideas are clear, specific, and well-developed. | Main ideas are identifiable, but may be somewhat general. | Main ideas are overly broad or simplistic. | Main ideas are unclear or not expressed. |
| **Organization** | Organization is clear (beginning, middle, and end) and fits the topic and writing form. | Organization is clear, but may be predictable or formulaic. | Organization is attempted, but is often unclear. | Organization is not coherent. |
| **Use of Details** | Details are relevant, specific, and well-placed. | Details are relevant, but may be overly general. | Details may be off-topic, predictable, or not specific enough. | Details are absent or insufficient to support main ideas. |
| **Vocabulary** | Vocabulary is exceptionally rich, varied, and well-chosen. | Vocabulary is colorful and generally avoids clichés. | Vocabulary is ordinary and may rely on clichés. | Vocabulary is limited, general, or vague. |
| **Mechanics and Usage** | Demonstrates exceptionally strong command of conventions of punctuation, capitalization, spelling, and usage. | Demonstrates control of conventions of punctuation, capitalization, spelling, and usage. | Errors in use of conventions of mechanics and usage distract, but do not impede, the reader. | Limited ability to control conventions of mechanics and usage impairs readability of the composition. |

# Proofreading Marks

Use these marks to show corrections.

| Mark | Meaning | Example |
|---|---|---|
| ⌿ | Take this out (delete). | I love t͠o to read. |
| ⊙ | Add a period. | It was late⊙ |
| ≡ | Make this a capital letter. | First prize went to m̲a̲r̲i̲a̲. |
| / | Make this a lowercase letter. | We saw a B̸lack C̸at. |
| ——— | Fix the spelling. | This is our h̶a̶u̶s̶e̶. (house) |
| ⋏ | Add a comma. | Goodnight⋏Mom. |
| ⋎ | Add an apostrophe. | That⋎s Lil⋎s bike. |
| ⋎ ⋎ | Add quotation marks. | ⋎Come in, he said.⋎ |
| !  ?  ⋏ ⋏ | Add an exclamation point or a question mark. | Help!⋏Can you help me?⋏ |
| ⋏ | Add a word. | The⋏pen is mine. (red) |
| ——— | Underline the words. | We read Old Yeller. |

EMC 2725 • Daily Paragraph Editing • ©2004 by Evan-Moor Corp.

**Editing Checklist**

Use this checklist to review and revise your writing:

| | |
|---|---|
| ◯ | Does each sentence begin with a capital letter? |
| ◯ | Do names of people and places begin with a capital letter? |
| ◯ | Does each sentence end with a period, a question mark, or an exclamation point? |
| ◯ | Did I use apostrophes to show possession (*Ana's desk*) and in contractions (*isn't*)? |
| ◯ | Did I choose the correct word (*to, too, two*)? |
| ◯ | Did I check for spelling errors? |
| ◯ | Did I place commas where they are needed? |
| ◯ | Are my sentences clear and complete? |

**Editing Checklist**

Use this checklist to review and revise your writing:

| | |
|---|---|
| ◯ | Does each sentence begin with a capital letter? |
| ◯ | Do names of people and places begin with a capital letter? |
| ◯ | Does each sentence end with a period, a question mark, or an exclamation point? |
| ◯ | Did I use apostrophes to show possession (*Ana's desk*) and in contractions (*isn't*)? |
| ◯ | Did I choose the correct word (*to, too, two*)? |
| ◯ | Did I check for spelling errors? |
| ◯ | Did I place commas where they are needed? |
| ◯ | Are my sentences clear and complete? |

Preview the 4 daily lessons to ensure you review or introduce skills that may be unfamiliar to students.

# Jane Goodall:
# Learning About Animals

what would your mother say if you took worms to bed ? what if you hid in a chicken house hous for hours ? a little girl growing up in england did these things. Her name was jane Goodall.

| Error Summary | |
| --- | --- |
| Capitalization | 5 |
| Punctuation: | |
| Period | 2 |
| Other | 2 |
| Spelling | 1 |

**MONDAY**                                    **WEEK 1**

jane goodall always loved animals. she slept with a toy chimpanzee when she was a baby. When Wen she was two, she hid earthworms under her pillow. she wanted to see what they did at night. when she was four, she hid in a chicken house until she saw a chicken lay an egg.

| Error Summary | |
| --- | --- |
| Capitalization | 5 |
| Punctuation: | |
| Period | 4 |
| Spelling | 1 |

**TUESDAY**                                    **WEEK 1**

Name —————————————————

# Jane Goodall:
# Learning About Animals

what would your mother say if you took worms to bed. what if you hid in a chicken hous for hours. a little girl growing up in england did these things Her name was jane Goodall

- names of people and places
- question marks

---

**MONDAY**                                          **WEEK 1**

---

jane goodall always loved animals she slept with a toy chimpanzee when she was a baby Wen she was two, she hid earthworms under her pillow she wanted to see what they did at night. when she was four, she hid in a chicken house until she saw a chicken lay an egg

- names of people

---

**TUESDAY**                                          **WEEK 1**

jane goodall went to africa when she grew up. She wanted to learn more about animals. she began watching chimpanzees in tanzania. She waited and ~~wached~~ watched until the chimps were not afraid of her.

| Error Summary | |
| --- | --- |
| Capitalization | 5 |
| Punctuation: | |
| 　Period | 4 |
| Spelling | 1 |

**WEDNESDAY**　　　　　**WEEK 1**

jane goodall watched chimpanzees for many years. she saw baby chimps grow up and start families of their own. She knew each chimp when she saw it. jane helped scientists learn ~~mor~~ more about the way animals behave by watching chimps for many years.

| Error Summary | |
| --- | --- |
| Capitalization | 4 |
| Punctuation: | |
| 　Period | 4 |
| Spelling | 1 |

**THURSDAY**　　　　　**WEEK 1**

jane goodall went to africa when she grew up She wanted to learn more about animals she began watching chimpanzees in tanzania She waited and wached until the chimps were not afraid of her

- names of people and places

**WEDNESDAY**                                   **WEEK 1**

jane goodall watched chimpanzees for many years she saw baby chimps grow up and start families of their own She knew each chimp when she saw it jane helped scientists learn mor about the way animals behave by watching chimps for many years

- names of people

**THURSDAY**                                   **WEEK 1**

**EDITING KEY:** Social Studies Article     **Daily Paragraph Editing**

Preview the 4 daily lessons to ensure you review or introduce skills that may be unfamiliar to students.

# Places on Earth

We live on a planet covered with land and water. You can only see a small part of our planet when you use your eyes to look around you. Maps, globes, and pictures can help you to see ~~sea~~ other places on Earth. Can you see where your home is on a map of Earth?

**MONDAY**     **WEEK 2**

There are many ways, to tell someone about where you live. You can tell someone the name of your town ~~toun~~. you might live in a big city like San francisco. Your city is also in a state. if you live in san Francisco, then you also live in the state of california.

**TUESDAY**     **WEEK 2**

# Places on Earth

    We live on a planet covered with land and water. You can only see a small part of our planet when you use your eyes to look around you. Maps globes and pictures can help you to sea other places on Earth. Can you see where your home is on a map of Earth

| MONDAY | WEEK 2 |
|---|---|

    There are many ways. to tell someone about where you live. You can tell someone the name of your toun. you might live in a big city like San francisco. Your city is also in a state. if you live in san Francisco, then you also live in the state of california

| TUESDAY | WEEK 2 |
|---|---|

states
Many ~~stats~~ together form a country. California is in the country called the United states of America. Canada and mexico are also countries. They are America's neighbors. These three countries are each part of one big piece of land? It is called a continent.

**Error Summary**

| | |
|---|---|
| Capitalization | 2 |
| Punctuation: | |
| Period | 1 |
| Spelling | 1 |

**WEDNESDAY**     **WEEK 2**

There
~~Their~~ are seven continents on Earth. The united states of America is located on the continent of North America. Earths six other continents are Africa, antarctica, Asia, australia, Europe, and South america. The rest of Earth is covered by water.

**Error Summary**

| | |
|---|---|
| Capitalization | 5 |
| Punctuation: | |
| Apostrophe | 1 |
| Comma | 2 |
| Spelling | 1 |

**THURSDAY**     **WEEK 2**

Many stats together form a country. California is in the country called the United states of America. Canada and mexico are also countries. They are America's neighbors. These three countries are each part of one big piece of land? It is called a continent.

- names of places

**WEDNESDAY**                                    **WEEK 2**

Their are seven continents on Earth. The united states of America is located on the continent of North America. Earths six other continents are Africa, antarctica Asia australia, Europe, and South america. The rest of Earth is covered by water.

- names of places
- commas

**THURSDAY**                                    **WEEK 2**

Preview the 4 daily lessons to ensure you review or introduce skills that may be unfamiliar to students.

# A Strong Heart

body

<u>e</u>xercise is good for your ~~bodie~~. <u>t</u>here

are many ways to exercise. You can exercise

indoors or outside⊙ <u>y</u>ou can exercise with

your friends when you play tag, soccer, or

basketball. You can exercise by yourself when

you ride your bike∧ jump rope∧ or swim laps⊙

**Error Summary**

| | |
|---|---|
| Capitalization | 3 |
| Punctuation: | |
|    Comma | 2 |
|    Period | 2 |
| Spelling | 1 |

**MONDAY**      **WEEK 3**

---

<u>a</u>s you read this, try to feel your heart

beating. <u>p</u>ut your pointer and middle fingers on

your jawbone near your ear. <u>r</u>un your fingers

your

down ~~you~~ neck until you feel your pulse. You

little

will feel a ~~littel~~ push each time your heart

beats

beats⊙ Count the ~~beets~~ for 15 seconds⊙

**Error Summary**

| | |
|---|---|
| Capitalization | 3 |
| Language Usage | 1 |
| Punctuation: | |
|    Period | 2 |
| Spelling | 2 |

**TUESDAY**      **WEEK 3**

# A Strong Heart

• commas

exercise is good for your bodie. there are many ways to exercise. You can exercise indoors or outside you can exercise with your friends when you play tag, soccer, or basketball. You can exercise by yourself when you ride your bike jump rope or swim laps

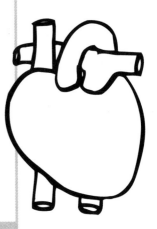

| MONDAY | WEEK 3 |
|---|---|

as you read this, try to feel your heart beating. put your pointer and middle fingers on your jawbone near your ear. run your fingers down you neck until you feel your pulse. You will feel a littel push each time your heart beats Count the beets for 15 seconds

| TUESDAY | WEEK 3 |
|---|---|

©2004 by Evan-Moor Corp. • Daily Paragraph Editing, Grade 2 • EMC 2725

How many times did you feel your heart beat? it should beat about once every second. When you finish reading this, stand up. Jump up and down for ~~won~~ one minute. then count your heartbeats for 15 seconds. what do you think will happen to the number of beats?

| Error Summary | |
| --- | --- |
| Capitalization | 3 |
| Punctuation: | |
|    Period | 2 |
|    Other | 2 |
| Spelling | 1 |

**WEDNESDAY**          **WEEK 3**

when you exercise, your heart beats faster. Your ~~hart~~ heart is a muscle. when it beats faster, it gets stronger. It even grows a little! you should exercise at least three days each week for 20 to 30 minutes at a time. get up and do something. make your heart stronger!

| Error Summary | |
| --- | --- |
| Capitalization | 5 |
| Punctuation: | |
|    Period | 2 |
| Spelling | 1 |

**THURSDAY**          **WEEK 3**

Name _____

How many times did you feel your heart beat it should beat about once every second When you finish reading this, stand up Jump up and down for won minute. then count your heartbeats for 15 seconds. what do you think will happen to the number of beats.

| WEDNESDAY | WEEK 3 |

when you exercise, your heart beats faster. Your hart is a muscle when it beats faster, it gets stronger. It even grows a little! you should exercise at least three days each week for 20 to 30 minutes at a time. get up and do something make your heart stronger!

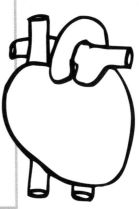

| THURSDAY | WEEK 3 |

Preview the 4 daily lessons to ensure you review or introduce skills that may be unfamiliar to students.

# My Kite

Hi. My name is maggie. I've always wanted a kite. I didn't want to buy one at the ~~stor~~ store. I wanted to make my own kite. I'm great at making things. Last march, i made a bird feeder. It's still hanging in the yard. This spring, I plan to make a kite.

**Error Summary**

| | |
|---|---|
| Capitalization | 3 |
| Punctuation: | |
|    Apostrophe | 4 |
| Spelling | 1 |

**MONDAY**                                         **WEEK 4**

Mom said i had to earn the money to buy the things I needed for my kite. I'm used to helping mom at home. To earn the ~~munney~~ money, I washed dishes on tuesday, played with my little brother on wednesday, and gave the dog a bath on friday. I'm good at all those things.

**Error Summary**

| | |
|---|---|
| Capitalization | 5 |
| Punctuation: | |
|    Apostrophe | 2 |
| Spelling | 1 |

**TUESDAY**                                         **WEEK 4**

EMC 2725 • Daily Paragraph Editing, Grade 2 • ©2004 by Evan-Moor Corp.

# My Kite

Hi. My name is maggie. Ive always wanted a kite. I didnt want to buy one at the stor. I wanted to make my own kite. Im great at making things. Last march, i made a bird feeder. Its still hanging in the yard. This spring, I plan to make a kite.

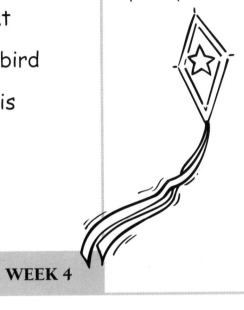

- names of people and months
- apostrophes

**MONDAY**        **WEEK 4**

Mom said i had to earn the money to buy the things I needed for my kite. Im used to helping mom at home. To earn the munney, I washed dishes on tuesday, played with my little brother on wednesday, and gave the dog a bath on friday. Im good at all those things.

- names of people and days of the week
- apostrophes

**TUESDAY**        **WEEK 4**

Finally, i had all the money I needed. I went to the craft shop on saturday. I bought paper, wood, glue, and kite string. When I got home, i thought about the right way to make the kite. I drew a plan for the kite, and then i went to worc.
work

### Error Summary

| | |
|---|---|
| Capitalization | 4 |
| Punctuation: | |
|   Comma | 2 |
| Spelling | 1 |

**WEDNESDAY**            **WEEK 4**

On Sunday, the kite was done. Wow! It looked great? I raced to the park to try it out. The wind was just right. I took a runing start and up the kite went it soared high in the sky I cheered, my little brother clapped, and even my dog seemed to jump for joy
running

### Error Summary

| | |
|---|---|
| Capitalization | 1 |
| Punctuation: | |
|   Period | 4 |
|   Other | 1 |
| Spelling | 1 |

**THURSDAY**            **WEEK 4**

Name _____

Finally, i had all the money I needed. I went to the craft shop on saturday. I bought paper wood, glue and kite string. When I got home, i thought about the right way to make the kite. I drew a plan for the kite, and then i went to worc.

- names of days of the week
- commas

**WEDNESDAY**　　　　　　　　　　**WEEK 4**

On Sunday, the kite was done. Wow. It looked great? I raced to the park to try it out. The wind was just right. I took a runing start and up the kite went it soared high in the sky I cheered, my little brother clapped, and even my dog seemed to jump for joy

- exclamation points

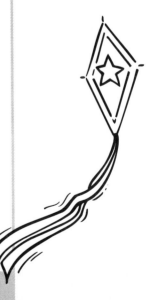

**THURSDAY**　　　　　　　　　　**WEEK 4**

Preview the 4 daily lessons to ensure you review or introduce skills that may be unfamiliar to students.

# Life in a Castle

Long ago in Europe, kings and nobles lived in castles. nobles were rich and powerful. The castles helped keep them safe from ~~there~~ their enemies. Some castles were near water⊙ Others were high on a mountain. from there, a guard could see ~~a~~ an enemy coming⊙

| Error Summary | |
|---|---|
| Capitalization | 2 |
| Language Usage | 1 |
| Punctuation: | |
| Period | 2 |
| Spelling | 1 |

**MONDAY**                                        **WEEK 5**

Most castles had a great hall where the noble family ate and had ~~partys~~ parties. There were also kitchens, bedrooms, and a chapel. Many ~~peoples~~ people worked in the castle. horses, chickens, pigs, and many other animals were also ~~keeped~~ kept there.

| Error Summary | |
|---|---|
| Capitalization | 1 |
| Language Usage | 1 |
| Punctuation: | |
| Comma | 2 |
| Spelling | 2 |

**TUESDAY**                                       **WEEK 5**

# Life in a Castle

Long ago in Europe, kings and nobles lived in castles. nobles were rich and powerful. The castles helped keep them safe from there enemies. Some castles were near water Others were high on a mountain. from there, a guard could see a enemy coming

---

---

Most castles had a great hall where the noble family ate and had partys. There were also kitchens, bedrooms, and a chapel. Many peoples worked in the castle. horses, chickens pigs and many other animals were also keeped there.

- commas

---

Some people ~~wishes~~ wish they could live in a huge castle. But life in a castle wasn't so ~~grate~~ great. The only light in the castle came from candles. there were only a few fireplaces to heat the rooms. In the winter, castles ~~was~~ were cold, damp, and dark.

**Error Summary**

| | |
|---|---|
| Capitalization | 1 |
| Language Usage | 2 |
| Punctuation: | |
| Apostrophe | 1 |
| Comma | 1 |
| Period | 2 |
| Spelling | 1 |

**WEDNESDAY**                                    **WEEK 5**

Many ~~castle~~ castles still stand in europe. You can go there and visit some of them. It's fun to imagine what castle ~~live~~ life was like. You can think about the rich nobles who lived there. You can also think about what things you might like about living in a castle.

**Error Summary**

| | |
|---|---|
| Capitalization | 1 |
| Language Usage | 1 |
| Punctuation: | |
| Apostrophe | 1 |
| Period | 3 |
| Spelling | 1 |

**THURSDAY**                                    **WEEK 5**

Some people wishes they could live in a huge castle. But life in a castle wasnt so grate The only light in the castle came from candles. there were only a few fireplaces to heat the rooms. In the winter, castles was cold damp, and dark

- apostrophes
- commas

**WEDNESDAY**                                    **WEEK 5**

Many castle still stand in europe. You can go there and visit some of them. Its fun to imagine what castle live was like You can think about the rich nobles who lived there You can also think about what things you might like about living in a castle

- apostrophes

**THURSDAY**                                        **WEEK 5**

Preview the 4 daily lessons to ensure you review or introduce skills that may be unfamiliar to students.

# It's Snowing!

Have you ever seen snow? Not everybody has. That's because some places do not get snow. austin, texas, is one place where it rarely snows. Other places, like aspen, colorado, get a lot of snow. In aspen, snow can fall at any time from october to may.

| Error Summary | |
|---|---|
| Capitalization | 7 |
| Punctuation: | |
|   Apostrophe | 1 |
|   Comma | 2 |
|   Period | 1 |
|   Other | 1 |

**MONDAY**        **WEEK 6**

---

Where does all the snow come from? It comes from clouds? Clouds are made of tiny drops of water. When these drops of water freeze, snowflakes form. the snowflakes get bigger and heavier. Then they fall to the ground.

| Error Summary | |
|---|---|
| Capitalization | 1 |
| Punctuation: | |
|   Period | 4 |
|   Other | 1 |

**TUESDAY**        **WEEK 6**

# It's Snowing!

Have you ever seen snow. Not everybody has. Thats because some places do not get snow austin texas, is one place where it rarely snows. Other places, like aspen colorado, get a lot of snow. In aspen, snow can fall at any time from october to may.

**MONDAY**                                **WEEK 6**

---

Where does all the snow come from. It comes from clouds? Clouds are made of tiny drops of water When these drops of water freeze, snowflakes form the snowflakes get bigger and heavier. Then they fall to the ground

**TUESDAY**                               **WEEK 6**

Snowflakes melt when they hit warm

ground

~~grouwnd~~. This is what happens in austin, texas.

Snow stays on ground that is cold. In aspen,

Colorado, the ground, trees, and rooftops get

covered with a blanket of white.

**Error Summary**

| Capitalization | 3 |
| --- | --- |
| Punctuation: | |
| Comma | 4 |
| Period | 1 |
| Spelling | 1 |

**WEDNESDAY**                                     **WEEK 6**

Snowflakes have six sides. Most snowflakes

two

are flat. No ~~too~~ look just alike. If it snows

where you live, catch two snowflakes on a piece

paper

of black ~~papper~~. Look at them, before they

melt. Can you count the six sides? Can you find

two snowflakes that look alike?

**Error Summary**

| Punctuation: | |
| --- | --- |
| Period | 2 |
| Other | 2 |
| Spelling | 2 |

**THURSDAY**                                      **WEEK 6**

Snowflakes melt when they hit warm grouwnd. This is what happens in austin texas. Snow stays on ground that is cold In aspen Colorado, the ground trees and rooftops get covered with a blanket of white.

- names of places
- commas

**WEDNESDAY**                                    **WEEK 6**

Snowflakes have six sides Most snowflakes are flat. No too look just alike. If it snows where you live, catch two snowflakes on a piece of black papper. Look at them. before they melt. Can you count the six sides. Can you find two snowflakes that look alike

- question marks

**THURSDAY**                                    **WEEK 6**

Preview the 4 daily lessons to ensure you review or introduce skills that may be unfamiliar to students.

# Beavers at Work

Beavers are mammals⊙They breathe air, but they spend a lot of time underwater⊙ beavers live in rivers and streams. They work in groups to block up ~~streems~~ streams and create ponds⊙They build their homes in these ponds. Beavers⌄ bodies help them work and swim⊙

| Error Summary | |
|---|---|
| Capitalization | 1 |
| Punctuation: | |
|   Apostrophe | 1 |
|   Period | 4 |
| Spelling | 1 |

**MONDAY**                                        **WEEK 7**

---

Beavers can close off their nose⌃ears, and throat to keep water out. they have see-through eyelids so they can see underwater⊙ Beavers⌄ flat tails and webbed back feet help them steer⌄ ~~And~~ swim in the water. ~~There~~ Their large front teeth can cut down trees⊙

| Error Summary | |
|---|---|
| Capitalization | 2 |
| Punctuation: | |
|   Apostrophe | 1 |
|   Comma | 1 |
|   Period | 3 |
| Spelling | 1 |

**TUESDAY**                                       **WEEK 7**

# Beavers at Work

Beavers are mammals They breathe air, but they spend a lot of time underwater beavers live in rivers and streams. They work in groups to block up streems and create ponds They build their homes in these ponds. Beavers bodies help them work and swim

• apostrophes

**MONDAY**　　　　　　　　　　**WEEK 7**

Beavers can close off their nose ears, and throat to keep water out. they have see-through eyelids so they can see underwater Beavers flat tails and webbed back feet help them steer. And swim in the water. There large front teeth can cut down trees

• apostrophes
• commas

**TUESDAY**　　　　　　　　　　**WEEK 7**

Beavers work together to build a dam⊙
First, they cut down ~~treas.~~ *trees* Next, they gnaw the trees into smaller pieces, drag them into the water, and pile them up. ̲beavers then scoop up mud with their front paws⊙They use the mud to fill in the spaces, ̸Between the branches⊙

### Error Summary

| Capitalization | 2 |
|---|---|
| Punctuation: | |
| Period | 4 |
| Spelling | 1 |

**WEDNESDAY**                                    **WEEK 7**

Water gathers behind the dam, and makes a pond. The beavers build their home in the pond⊙The beavers ̌home looks like a big pile of sticks on the outside⊙ ̲it is hollow inside. There is a ledge above the water where the beavers can sleep. ~~There~~ *Their* door is underwater.

### Error Summary

| Capitalization | 1 |
|---|---|
| Punctuation: | |
| Apostrophe | 1 |
| Period | 3 |
| Spelling | 1 |

**THURSDAY**                                    **WEEK 7**

EMC 2725 • Daily Paragraph Editing, Grade 2 • ©2004 by Evan-Moor Corp.

Beavers work together to build a dam First, they cut down treas. Next, they gnaw the trees into smaller pieces, drag them into the water, and pile them up. beavers then scoop up mud with their front paws They use the mud to fill in the spaces. Between the branches

**WEDNESDAY**                                         **WEEK 7**

Water gathers behind the dam. and makes a pond. The beavers build their home in the pond The beavers home looks like a big pile of sticks on the outside it is hollow inside. There is a ledge above the water where the beavers can sleep. There door is underwater.

• apostrophes

6 errors

**THURSDAY**                                         **WEEK 7**

Preview the 4 daily lessons to ensure you review or introduce skills that may be unfamiliar to students.

# Noises in the Night

Jamal sat up in bed. he heard noises on the roof. Was someone trying to break into the house? "mom! Dad!" shouted Jamal as he ran into his parent's bedroom. "did you hear that noise? What is it? Just then, there was a loud crash in the backyard.

| Error Summary | |
|---|---|
| Capitalization | 3 |
| Punctuation: | |
| Apostrophe | 1 |
| Period | 2 |
| Quotation Mark | 1 |
| Other | 2 |

**MONDAY**                    **WEEK 8**

Something had been knocked over. In the backyard. "I think I know what it is," Dad said. He grabbed a flashlight and hurried out the back door. "I was right," said dad as he shined the light on a raccoon. it was standing by the overturned garbage can.

| Error Summary | |
|---|---|
| Capitalization | 3 |
| Punctuation: | |
| Period | 2 |
| Quotation Mark | 2 |

**TUESDAY**                    **WEEK 8**

Name _____

# Noises in the Night

Jamal sat up in bed he heard noises on the roof. Was someone trying to break into the house. "mom! Dad!" shouted Jamal as he ran into his parent's bedroom. "did you hear that noise What is it? Just then, there was a loud crash in the backyard

- dialog
- question marks

---

**MONDAY**                                                    **WEEK 8**

---

Something had been knocked over. In the backyard. "I think I know what it is, Dad said. He grabbed a flashlight and hurried out the back door. I was right," said dad as he shined the light on a raccoon. it was standing by the overturned garbage can

- dialog

---

**TUESDAY**                                                   **WEEK 8**

---

"scat, you pesky raccoon! shouted Dad. In the wink of an eye, the animal was gone. Raccoons are wild animals," dad said. "they come into town trying to find food. They use their paws like hands. they can even take the lid off the garbage can to look for food.

| Error Summary | |
|---|---|
| Capitalization | 4 |
| Punctuation: | |
| Quotation Mark | 3 |

**WEDNESDAY**                    **WEEK 8**

As jamal helped clean up the mess, dad told him more about raccoons. "they look cute, but they can be dangerous," he said. "never feed one or try to pet it. We'll put hooks on the garbage can lid. That should keep him out. Now, let's go get some sleep.

| Error Summary | |
|---|---|
| Capitalization | 4 |
| Punctuation: | |
| Quotation Mark | 1 |
| Spelling | 1 |

**THURSDAY**                    **WEEK 8**

"scat, you pesky raccoon! shouted Dad. In the wink of an eye, the animal was gone. Raccoons are wild animals," dad said. "they come into town trying to find food. They use their paws like hands. they can even take the lid off the garbage can to look for food.

• dialog

**WEDNESDAY**                    **WEEK 8**

As jamal helped clean up the mess, dad told him more about raccoons. "they look cute, but they can be dangerous," he said. "never feed one or try to pet it. We'll put hooks on the garbage can lid. That should keep him out. Now, let's go get some sleap.

• dialog

6 errors

**THURSDAY**                    **WEEK 8**

Preview the 4 daily lessons to ensure you review or introduce skills that may be unfamiliar to students.

# My Dog Max

My dog max is a terrific dog. He can fetch sticks. And perform many tricks. The only bad thing about max is mud. He loves it. He plays in mud puddles after it rains. He dig holes in the garden soil. I yell max, no!" But max just keeps wagging his tail and digging.

_digs_

**Error Summary**

| Capitalization | 5 |
| Language Usage | 1 |
| Punctuation: | |
| Comma | 1 |
| Period | 2 |
| Quotation Mark | 1 |

**MONDAY**                    **WEEK 9**

I got home from school at 300 this afternoon. As usual, max came running to greet me. He had mud from the top of his hed to the tip of his tail. I said, "max, you are a mess. Max's tail stopped wagging because he knew he was in trouble. I said, Max, you need a bath."

_running_

_head_

**Error Summary**

| Capitalization | 2 |
| Punctuation: | |
| Comma | 1 |
| Period | 1 |
| Quotation Mark | 2 |
| Other | 1 |
| Spelling | 2 |

**TUESDAY**                    **WEEK 9**

EMC 2725 • Daily Paragraph Editing, Grade 2 • ©2004 by Evan-Moor Corp.

# My Dog Max

- dialog

My dog max is a terrific dog. He can fetch sticks. And perform many tricks. The only bad thing about max is mud. He loves it He plays in mud puddles after it rains. He dig holes in the garden soil. I yell max, no!" But max just keeps wagging his tail and digging.

**MONDAY**                                          **WEEK 9**

I got home from school at 300 this afternoon. As usual, max came runing to greet me. He had mud from the top of his hed to the tip of his tail. I said "max, you are a mess. Max's tail stopped wagging. because he knew he was in trouble. I said, Max, you need a bath."

- colons in time
- dialog

**TUESDAY**                                          **WEEK 9**

He loves getting dirty, but max hates getting clean. When I got the ~~sop~~ soap, the tub, and the hose, max took off! I chased him all over. At last, I grabbed him. I had to drag him to the tub. I yelled, "come on, max. Get in the tub! Finally, at 400, max was in the tub.

**Error Summary**

| | |
|---|---|
| Capitalization | 5 |
| Punctuation: | |
|   Comma | 1 |
|   Period | 1 |
|   Quotation Mark | 1 |
|   Other | 1 |
| Spelling | 1 |

**WEDNESDAY**           **WEEK 9**

I rubbed soap all over max, rinsed it off, and dried him with a towel. I told him, "you look great. Now stay out of the mud. Max ran off. I put the soap, tub, and hose away. I looked ~~four~~ max and found him rolling in the mud. I yelled, "max, it's only 430!"

**Error Summary**

| | |
|---|---|
| Capitalization | 4 |
| Punctuation: | |
|   Comma | 1 |
|   Quotation Mark | 1 |
|   Other | 1 |
| Spelling | 1 |

**THURSDAY**           **WEEK 9**

EMC 2725 • Daily Paragraph Editing, Grade 2 • ©2004 by Evan-Moor Corp.

He loves getting dirty, but max hates getting clean. When I got the sop, the tub, and the hose, max took off! I chased him all over. At last, I grabbed him. I had to drag him to the tub I yelled "come on, max. Get in the tub! Finally, at 400, max was in the tub.

**WATCH FOR**

- colons in time
- dialog

**WEDNESDAY**                                    **WEEK 9**

I rubbed soap all over max, rinsed it off, and dried him with a towel. I told him "you look great. Now stay out of the mud. Max ran off. I put the soap, tub, and hose away. I looked four max and found him rolling in the mud. I yelled, "max, it's only 430!"

**WATCH FOR**

- colons in time
- dialog

**THURSDAY**                                    **WEEK 9**

Preview the 4 daily lessons to ensure you review or introduce skills that may be unfamiliar to students.

# A Message from Uncle Wilbur

Our uncle wilbur is a little strange. We can't ever tell what he'll send us. Last ~~sundae~~ Sunday, he sent us a box. It was full of holes, and covered with messages. Inside the box, we found a goldfish in a bowl and a letter.

Here's what the letter said:

**Error Summary**

| | |
|---|---|
| Capitalization | 3 |
| Punctuation: | |
| Apostrophe | 2 |
| Period | 1 |
| Spelling | 1 |

**MONDAY**                    **WEEK 10**

---

Dear sarah and Sid,

Please

~~Pleese~~ take care of my pet goldfish, oscar, while Im away. Talk to him. he likes it. See you on friday.

Love,

Uncle wilbur

**Error Summary**

| | |
|---|---|
| Capitalization | 5 |
| Punctuation: | |
| Apostrophe | 1 |
| Comma | 2 |
| Spelling | 1 |

**TUESDAY**                    **WEEK 10**

# A Message from Uncle Wilbur

Our uncle wilbur is a little strange. We cant ever tell what he'll send us. Last sundae, he sent us a box. It was full of holes. and covered with messages. Inside the box, we found a goldfish in a bowl and a letter.

Heres what the letter said:

**WATCH FOR**

- names of people and days of the week
- apostrophes

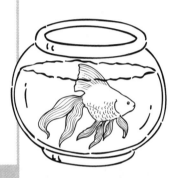

| MONDAY | WEEK 10 |
|---|---|

Dear sarah and Sid

Pleese take care of my pet goldfish, oscar, while Im away. Talk to him. he likes it. See you on friday.

Love

Uncle wilbur

**WATCH FOR**

- names of people and pets
- commas
- apostrophes

| TUESDAY | WEEK 10 |
|---|---|

uncle Wilbur came to take Oscar home on friday. Wel'l miss him, but uncle Wilbur left us another box. He sed "this is your thank-you present. the box had holes in the top. It was very heavy, and it hissed.

| Error Summary | |
|---|---|
| Capitalization | 5 |
| Punctuation: | |
| Apostrophe | 1 |
| Comma | 1 |
| Quotation Mark | 1 |
| Spelling | 1 |

**WEDNESDAY** · **WEEK 10**

A message on the box said, "don't poke fingers in holes!

I dont want to open it," whispered Sid.

Ill do it," said Sarah. She slowly lifted off the lid. She looked in the box. "Eeeeeek! she screamed.

| Error Summary | |
|---|---|
| Capitalization | 1 |
| Punctuation: | |
| Apostrophe | 2 |
| Quotation Mark | 4 |

**THURSDAY** · **WEEK 10**

EMC 2725 • Daily Paragraph Editing, Grade 2 • ©2004 by Evan-Moor Corp.

Name _____

uncle Wilbur came to take Oscar home on friday. Wel'l miss him, but uncle Wilbur left us another box. He sed "this is your thank-you present. the box had holes in the top. It was very heavy, and it hissed.

WATCH FOR

- names of people and days of the week
- commas
- apostrophes
- dialog

A message on the box said, "don't poke fingers in holes!

I dont want to open it," whispered Sid.

Ill do it," said Sarah. She slowly lifted off the lid. She looked in the box. "Eeeeeek! she screamed.

WATCH FOR

- apostrophes
- dialog

Preview the 4 daily lessons to ensure you review or introduce skills that may be unfamiliar to students.

# Pen Pals

Kevin quickly opened his letter from his pen pal, ramon. He lives far away from Kevin in the Dominican republic. The letter said:

Dear kevin

My ~~teem~~ won a baseball game.
team
Im the catcher.

| Error Summary | |
|---|---|
| Capitalization | 3 |
| Punctuation: | |
| Apostrophe | 1 |
| Comma | 1 |
| Spelling | 1 |

**MONDAY**                                    **WEEK 11**

Were about to eat Moms famous chicken stew with plantains. A plantain is a kind of banana I hope I get a chicken foot in my stew. I also hope you ~~rite~~ soon.
write

Your Friend

ramon

| Error Summary | |
|---|---|
| Capitalization | 2 |
| Punctuation: | |
| Apostrophe | 2 |
| Comma | 1 |
| Period | 1 |
| Spelling | 1 |

**TUESDAY**                                    **WEEK 11**

# Pen Pals

Kevin quickly opened his letter from his pen pal, ramon. He lives far away from Kevin in the Dominican republic. The letter said:

Dear kevin

My teem won a baseball game. Im the catcher.

**MONDAY**                                    **WEEK 11**

- commas
- names of people and places

Dear

---

Were about to eat Moms famous chicken stew with plantains. A plantain is a kind of banana I hope I get a chicken foot in my stew. I also hope you rite soon.

Your Friend

ramon

- commas
- names of people
- apostrophes

**TUESDAY**                                   **WEEK 11**

kevin got a pencil and some paper. He wrote:

Dear, Ramon

    I liked your letter. Did you get a chicken foot in your stew? My mom makes chicken stew, too. She hasnt ever put in chicken feet. What do they ~~tast~~ taste like?

| Error Summary | |
|---|---|
| Capitalization | 1 |
| Punctuation: | |
|   Apostrophe | 1 |
|   Comma | 2 |
|   Period | 1 |
|   Other | 1 |
| Spelling | 1 |

**WEDNESDAY**                                                        **WEEK 11**

    I'm glad your team ~~win~~ won the game. I play baseball, too. Im the pitcher. whats the name of your ~~teem~~ team? My teams name is Lightning. That's because we're fast!

    Your friend,

    Kevin

| Error Summary | |
|---|---|
| Capitalization | 1 |
| Language Usage | 1 |
| Punctuation: | |
|   Apostrophe | 3 |
|   Comma | 1 |
|   Period | 1 |
|   Other | 1 |
| Spelling | 1 |

**THURSDAY**                                                        **WEEK 11**

EMC 2725 • Daily Paragraph Editing, Grade 2 • ©2004 by Evan-Moor Corp.

kevin got a pencil and some paper. He wrote:

Dear, Ramon

I liked your letter Did you get a chicken foot in your stew. My mom makes chicken stew, too. She hasnt ever put in chicken feet. What do they tast like?

WATCH FOR

- commas
- question marks
- apostrophes

**WEDNESDAY** **WEEK 11**

I'm glad your team win the game I play baseball, too. Im the pitcher. whats' the name of your teem. My teams name is Lightning. That's because we're fast!

Your friend

Kevin

WATCH FOR

- commas
- question marks
- apostrophes

Dear

**THURSDAY** **WEEK 11**

Preview the 4 daily lessons to ensure you review or introduce skills that may be unfamiliar to students.

# A Great Book of Poems

I have been reading many books of poems for children⊙I have been looking for the best one. I just finished reading <u>Come Take a Walk</u>. It is a book of poems written by lisa boyd.

think
I ~~theenk~~ it is the best book of children's poems i have ever read.

**Error Summary**

| | |
|---|---|
| Capitalization | 3 |
| Punctuation: | |
| Apostrophe | 1 |
| Period | 1 |
| Other | 1 |
| Spelling | 1 |

**MONDAY**                     **WEEK 12**

Let me tell you about ms⊙Boyds book. The poems have titles like "Ice-Cream Dream" and Sticky Stacks of Flapjacks." Wow!The titles

read
made me want to ~~reed~~ the poems. I like a title like "stick man stan because it makes me laugh and want to keep on reading.

**Error Summary**

| | |
|---|---|
| Capitalization | 4 |
| Punctuation: | |
| Apostrophe | 1 |
| Period | 1 |
| Quotation Mark | 2 |
| Other | 1 |
| Spelling | 1 |

**TUESDAY**                     **WEEK 12**

EMC 2725 • Daily Paragraph Editing, Grade 2 • ©2004 by Evan-Moor Corp.

# A Great Book of Poems

I have been reading many books of poems for children I have been looking for the best one. I just finished reading Come Take a Walk. It is a book of poems written by lisa boyd. I theenk it is the best book of childrens poems i have ever read.

- titles of books
- names of people

**MONDAY**                              **WEEK 12**

Let me tell you about ms Boyds book. The poems have titles like "Ice-Cream Dream" and Sticky Stacks of Flapjacks." Wow The titles made me want to reed the poems. I like a title like "stick man stan because it makes me laugh and want to keep on reading.

WATCH FOR

- titles of poems
- names of people
- exclamation points

**TUESDAY**                              **WEEK 12**

lisa boyd has written many childrens books. Come Take a Walk is her latest. Ms boyd said she read her poems to children first. Then she chose the best ones for her book "creepy crawly Critters was one of their favorites. I think it was one of my favorites, ~~two~~ too.

| Error Summary | |
|---|---|
| Capitalization | 5 |
| Punctuation: | |
| Apostrophe | 1 |
| Period | 2 |
| Quotation Mark | 1 |
| Other | 1 |
| Spelling | 1 |

**WEDNESDAY**                    **WEEK 12**

If you have a pet, make sure you read Fido's fuzzy fur." Has a younger brother or sister ever bitten you? You can laugh about it when you read Ouch?! that hurt!" If you enjoy childrens poems, try this book. lisa boyd has a big hit with come take a walk.

| Error Summary | |
|---|---|
| Capitalization | 9 |
| Punctuation: | |
| Apostrophe | 1 |
| Quotation Mark | 2 |
| Other | 2 |

**THURSDAY**                    **WEEK 12**

EMC 2725 • Daily Paragraph Editing, Grade 2 • ©2004 by Evan-Moor Corp.

lisa boyd has written many childrens books. Come Take a Walk is her latest. Ms boyd said she read her poems to children first. Then she chose the best ones for her book "creepy crawly Critters was one of their favorites. I think it was one of my favorites, two.

WATCH FOR

- titles of books and poems
- names of people

**WEDNESDAY**      **WEEK 12**

---

If you have a pet, make sure you read Fido's fuzzy fur." Has a younger brother or sister ever bitten you? You can laugh about it when you read Ouch? that hurt!" If you enjoy childrens poems, try this book. lisa boyd has a big hit with come take a walk.

WATCH FOR

- titles of books and poems
- names of people
- exclamation points

**THURSDAY**      **WEEK 12**

Preview the 4 daily lessons to ensure you review or introduce skills that may be unfamiliar to students.

# Thanksgiving with Grandmarge

Some ~~peeple~~ (people) have a grandma. Others have a nana. I have Grandmarge. She is my dads mother. Her real name is marge, but to me she's Grandmarge. I dont get to see her much. Thats why thanksgiving is my favorite day of the year. I know I'll see her on that day.

**Error Summary**

| | |
|---|---|
| Capitalization | 2 |
| Punctuation: | |
| Apostrophe | 3 |
| Spelling | 1 |

**MONDAY**                                    **WEEK 13**

Each november, we make a trip to grandmarges house in Topeka, kansas. We usually go right after school at 300 on wednesday. When we get to Grandmarges ~~howse~~ (house), she throws her arms around me and pulls a piece of candy out of my ear?

**Error Summary**

| | |
|---|---|
| Capitalization | 4 |
| Punctuation: | |
| Apostrophe | 2 |
| Period | 1 |
| Other | 1 |
| Spelling | 1 |

**TUESDAY**                                    **WEEK 13**

EMC 2725 • Daily Paragraph Editing, Grade 2 • ©2004 by Evan-Moor Corp.

# Thanksgiving with Grandmarge

Some peeple have a grandma. Others have a nana. I have Grandmarge. She is my dads mother. Her real name is marge, but to me she's Grandmarge. I dont get to see her much. Thats why thanksgiving is my favorite day of the year. I know I'll see her on that day.

- names of people and holidays
- apostrophes

**MONDAY**                                    **WEEK 13**

Each november, we make a trip to grandmarges house in Topeka, kansas. We usually go right after school at 300 on wednesday. When we get to Grandmarges howse, she throws her arms around me and pulls a piece of candy out of my ear?

- names of people and places
- apostrophes
- colons in time

**TUESDAY**                                    **WEEK 13**

On wednesday night, Grandmarge tucks me into bed. It's my dads old bed with my favorite blew ~~blew~~ and white striped sheets. Then Grandmarge reads a poem. It's the same one every year. She says it was dads favorite. It's called "The Dirtiest Man in the World."

**Error Summary**

| | |
|---|---|
| Capitalization | 2 |
| Punctuation: | |
|   Apostrophe | 5 |
|   Period | 1 |
| Spelling | 1 |

**WEDNESDAY**        **WEEK 13**

---

When I wake up, the smell of turkey fills the air. I know that grandmarge has been cooking since early in the morning. Every ~~yeer~~ year at 12:00 sharp, she says, "It's thanksgiving! Lets eat. I thank you. You thank me. Please dont drop a single pea!"

**Error Summary**

| | |
|---|---|
| Capitalization | 2 |
| Punctuation: | |
|   Apostrophe | 3 |
|   Period | 1 |
|   Other | 1 |
| Spelling | 1 |

**THURSDAY**        **WEEK 13**

On wednesday night, Grandmarge tucks me into bed. Its my dads old bed with my favorite blew and white striped sheets. Then Grandmarge reads a poem Its the same one every year. She says it was dads favorite. Its called "The Dirtiest Man in the World."

• apostrophes

**WEDNESDAY**                    **WEEK 13**

When I wake up, the smell of turkey fills the air. I know that grandmarge has been cooking since early in the morning Every yeer at 1200 sharp, she says, "Its thanksgiving! Lets eat. I thank you. You thank me. Please dont drop a single pea!"

• names of people and holidays

• colons in time

**THURSDAY**                    **WEEK 13**

Preview the 4 daily lessons to ensure you review or introduce skills that may be unfamiliar to students.

# Learning About Holidays

What holiday do we have in july? What do you know about the holiday kwanzaa? If you want to ~~lern~~ learn about these and other holidays, I have the book for you. holidays in america was written by john hall. it tells about holidays and how people honor them.

**Error Summary**

| | |
|---|---|
| Capitalization | 7 |
| Punctuation: | |
|   Other | 3 |
| Spelling | 1 |

**MONDAY**                                        **WEEK 14**

---

There are 12 chapters in Holidays in America. each one tells about the holidays in one ~~munth~~ month. The second chapter is about february's holidays. Did you know the third monday in february is Presidents' day? we honor all past presidents on that day.

**Error Summary**

| | |
|---|---|
| Capitalization | 6 |
| Punctuation: | |
|   Other | 2 |
| Spelling | 1 |

**TUESDAY**                                       **WEEK 14**

     EMC 2725 • Daily Paragraph Editing, Grade 2 • ©2004 by Evan-Moor Corp.

Name _____

# Learning About Holidays

What holiday do we have in july. What do you know about the holiday kwanzaa. If you want to lern about these and other holidays, I have the book for you. holidays in america was written by john hall. it tells about holidays and how people honor them.

**MONDAY**          **WEEK 14**

There are 12 chapters in Holidays in America. each one tells about the holidays in one munth. The second chapter is about february's holidays. Did you know the third monday in february is Presidents' day. we honor all past presidents on that day.

**TUESDAY**          **WEEK 14**

In his book, mr. hall tells about holidays that you may not know about. have you heard of juneteenth.?It is the oldest holiday to celebrate the end of slavery. it began in Galveston, Texas, in 1865. Today, people in many states remember this special day on june 19th.

**Error Summary**

| | |
|---|---|
| Capitalization | 6 |
| Punctuation: | |
| Comma | 1 |
| Period | 1 |
| Other | 1 |

**WEDNESDAY**                    **WEEK 14**

holidays in america is a great book. I like to eat holiday foods. I learned about potato pancakes for Hanukkah, corned beef and cabbage for Saint patrick's day, and many other holiday foods. If you want to know more about holidays, you should read mr. hall's book.

**Error Summary**

| | |
|---|---|
| Capitalization | 6 |
| Punctuation: | |
| Period | 1 |
| Other | 1 |
| Spelling | 1 |

**THURSDAY**                    **WEEK 14**

Name —————————————————————

In his book, mr hall tells about holidays that you may not know about. have you heard of juneteenth. It is the oldest holiday to celebrate the end of slavery. it began in Galveston Texas, in 1865. Today, people in many states remember this special day on june 19th.

WATCH FOR

- names of people, months, and holidays
- commas

**WEDNESDAY**                                    **WEEK 14**

holidays in america is a great book. I like to eet holiday foods. I learned about potato pancakes for Hanukkah, corned beef and cabbage for Saint patrick's day, and many other holiday foods. If you want to know more about holidays, you should read mr hall's book.

WATCH FOR

- names of people, books, and holidays

**THURSDAY**                                    **WEEK 14**

Preview the 4 daily lessons to ensure you review or introduce skills that may be unfamiliar to students.

# Weed Seeds

candy ran through the weeds in the vacant lot. morris chased after his dog. "Come here, candy," he called. candy turned and ran to morris. She waved her bushy tail back and forth through the tall weeds.

**Error Summary**

| | |
|---|---|
| Capitalization | 5 |
| Punctuation: | |
| Period | 1 |
| Quotation Mark | 1 |

**MONDAY**      **WEEK 15**

"Candy, you're (your) tail is a mess. Its full of stickers," morris said to his dog. He saw that his socks we're full of stickers, too. "Lets go home. Im going to have to pull all these stickers off us," he said to Candy.

**Error Summary**

| | |
|---|---|
| Capitalization | 1 |
| Punctuation: | |
| Apostrophe | 3 |
| Quotation Mark | 2 |
| Spelling | 2 |

**TUESDAY**      **WEEK 15**

EMC 2725 • Daily Paragraph Editing, Grade 2 • ©2004 by Evan-Moor Corp.

# Weed Seeds

candy ran through the weeds in the vacant lot. morris chased after his dog. Come here, candy," he called. candy turned and ran to morris She waved her bushy tail back and forth through the tall weeds.

- dialog
- names of people and pets

**MONDAY**                                **WEEK 15**

---

Candy, you're tail is a mess. Its full of stickers," morris said to his dog. He saw that his socks we're full of stickers, too. "Lets go home. Im going to have to pull all these stickers off us, he said to Candy.

- dialog
- apostrophes

**TUESDAY**                                **WEEK 15**

<u>m</u>orris was almost finished pulling off the stickers when his brother showed up. "Do you know what those are?" asked Jake." "Those stickers are plant seeds. I bet if we plant them in some dirt, wed grow a sticker plant in a few weeks.

**Error Summary**

| | |
|---|---|
| Capitalization | 1 |
| Punctuation: | |
|   Apostrophe | 1 |
|   Period | 1 |
|   Quotation Mark | 3 |

**WEDNESDAY**        **WEEK 15**

The boys took a handful of stikkers. _stickers_ They scattered them in a big pot of soil they covered the stickers. With more soil. Then they sprinkled them with water. "Now well just have to wait and water," said Jake."

**Error Summary**

| | |
|---|---|
| Capitalization | 2 |
| Punctuation: | |
|   Apostrophe | 1 |
|   Period | 2 |
|   Quotation Mark | 2 |
| Spelling | 1 |

**THURSDAY**        **WEEK 15**

Name _____

morris was almost finished pulling off the stickers when his brother showed up. "Do you know what those are? asked Jake." "Those stickers are plant seeds. I bet if we plant them in some dirt, wed grow a sticker plant in a few weeks

• dialog
• apostrophes

**WEDNESDAY**                                        **WEEK 15**

The boys took a handful of stikkers. They scattered them in a big pot of soil they covered the stickers. With more soil. Then they sprinkled them with water. "Now well just have to wait and water, said Jake."

• dialog
• apostrophes

**THURSDAY**                                        **WEEK 15**

Preview the 4 daily lessons to ensure you review or introduce skills that may be unfamiliar to students.

# Magnet Tricks

Magnet Madness is a book full of magnet tricks. A woman named ms. Maggie nett wrote it. What is a magnet? A magnet has a force you cannot see. it is called a magnetic force. The force pulls objects made of iron, steel, nickel, and other metals to the magnet.

| Error Summary | |
|---|---|
| Capitalization | 3 |
| Punctuation: | |
| Comma | 2 |
| Period | 1 |
| Other | 1 |

**MONDAY**                                   **WEEK 16**

Magnets come in different shapes, sizes, and strengths. There are bar magnets, square magnets, and U-shaped magnets. Some magnets are small. Do you have small magnets on your refrigerator? ms. netts book says huge magnets can pull things like trane cars.
train

| Error Summary | |
|---|---|
| Capitalization | 2 |
| Punctuation: | |
| Apostrophe | 1 |
| Comma | 2 |
| Period | 1 |
| Other | 1 |
| Spelling | 1 |

**TUESDAY**                                   **WEEK 16**

Name _____

# Magnet Tricks

<u>Magnet Madness</u> is a book full of magnet tricks. A woman named ms Maggie nett wrote it. What is a magnet. A magnet has a force you cannot see. it is called a magnetic force. The force pulls objects made of iron, steel nickel and other metals to the magnet.

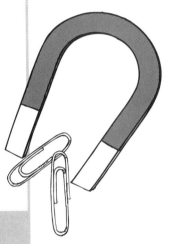

**MONDAY**                    **WEEK 16**

Magnets come in different shapes, sizes and strengths. There are bar magnets square magnets, and U-shaped magnets. Some magnets are small. Do you have small magnets on your refrigerator. ms netts book says huge magnets can pull things like trane cars.

**TUESDAY**                    **WEEK 16**

In magnet Madness, ms. nett tells about a way to see a magnet's unseen force. Place a piece of ~~payper~~ paper on top of a bar magnet. sprinkle iron shavings on top of the paper. the shavings will form a pattern. The pattern shows the lines in the magnetic field.

| Error Summary | |
|---|---|
| Capitalization | 5 |
| Punctuation: | |
|    Period | 4 |
| Spelling | 1 |

**WEDNESDAY**                              **WEEK 16**

A magnets force can go through objects. There is a trick in magnet madness that ~~showes~~ shows this. use a strong magnet to pick up one paper clip. pick up another paper clip with the end of the first one. keep picking up clips. How many clips can you pick up.?

| Error Summary | |
|---|---|
| Capitalization | 5 |
| Punctuation: | |
|    Apostrophe | 1 |
|    Period | 1 |
|    Other | 1 |
| Spelling | 1 |

**THURSDAY**                              **WEEK 16**

EMC 2725 • *Daily Paragraph Editing, Grade 2* • ©2004 by Evan-Moor Corp.

In <u>magnet Madness</u>, ms nett tells about a way to see a magnet's unseen force. Place a piece of payper on top of a bar magnet sprinkle iron shavings on top of the paper the shavings will form a pattern. The pattern shows the lines in the magnetic field

**WEDNESDAY**            **WEEK 16**

A magnets force can go through objects. There is a trick in <u>magnet madness</u> that showes this. use a strong magnet to pick up one paper clip. pick up another paper clip with the end of the first one keep picking up clips. How many clips can you pick up.

• question marks

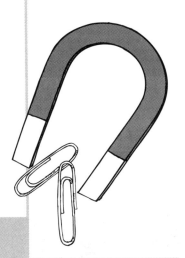

**THURSDAY**            **WEEK 16**

Preview the 4 daily lessons to ensure you review or introduce skills that may be unfamiliar to students.

# George Washington's Barn

George washington was an important man. He was a brave soldier and our ~~ferst~~ first president. Mr. washington was also a farmer. He studied farming and learned the best way to plant and harvest crops.

| Error Summary | |
|---|---|
| Capitalization | 2 |
| Punctuation: | |
|    Period | 3 |
| Spelling | 1 |

**MONDAY**                  **WEEK 17**

Wheat was one of the crops that mr. washington grew. The kernels of wheat are ground to make ~~flower~~ flour. Getting the kernels off the wheat stalk was a hard job. it took a lot of time. Mr. Washington wanted to make it easier to do this job.

| Error Summary | |
|---|---|
| Capitalization | 3 |
| Punctuation: | |
|    Period | 3 |
| Spelling | 1 |

**TUESDAY**                  **WEEK 17**

# George Washington's Barn

George washington was an important man. He was a brave soldier and our ferst president Mr washington was also a farmer. He studied farming and learned the best way to plant and harvest crops

**MONDAY**                                    **WEEK 17**

Wheat was one of the crops that mr washington grew. The kernels of wheat are ground to make flower. Getting the kernels off the wheat stalk was a hard job it took a lot of time. Mr Washington wanted to make it easier to do this job.

**TUESDAY**                                    **WEEK 17**

He built a special barn with 16 sides. the barn was on a hill with a ramp to the door. There was a basement underneath the barn. The wheat was cut, And spread on the floor of the barn. two mules walked up the ramp into the barn. They walked around on the wheat.

| Error Summary | |
| --- | --- |
| Capitalization | 3 |
| Punctuation: | |
| Period | 4 |
| Spelling | 1 |

**WEDNESDAY**

**WEEK 17**

When the mules walked on the wheat, the kernels came off the stalks. the kernels fell through holes in the floor to the basement. workers in the basement swept up the kernels. The kernels could be ground to make flour for bread. Mr. washingtons plan worked well.

| Error Summary | |
| --- | --- |
| Capitalization | 3 |
| Punctuation: | |
| Apostrophe | 1 |
| Period | 2 |
| Spelling | 1 |

**THURSDAY**

**WEEK 17**

EMC 2725 • Daily Paragraph Editing, Grade 2 • ©2004 by Evan-Moor Corp.

Name _____

He built a special barn with 16 sides the barn was on a hill with a ramp to the door. There was a basement underneath the barn The wheat was cut. And spread on the floor of the barn. two mules walked up the ramp into the barn. They walked around on the wheet

**WEDNESDAY**                                          **WEEK 17**

---

When the mules walked on the wheat, the kernels came off the stalks the kernels fell through holes in the floor to the basement. workers in the basement swept up the kernels. The kernels could be ground to make flour for bred. Mr washingtons plan worked well.

• titles of people

**THURSDAY**                                          **WEEK 17**

Preview the 4 daily lessons to ensure you review or introduce skills that may be unfamiliar to students.

# Holiday Gifts

You can make a flag, For a valentine's Day gift. You need 18 in. of fabric for the flag. You also need fabric scraps, paint, and glue. First, make a design using paint and scraps. Next, find a stick that is 3 ft. long. roll the end of the flag around the stick and glue it in place.

**Error Summary**

| | |
|---|---|
| Capitalization | 3 |
| Punctuation: | |
| Comma | 1 |
| Period | 4 |

**MONDAY**                                        **WEEK 18**

To make a may Day basket, get a green plastic strawberry basket, a ribbon that's 12 in. long, and 8 pieces of yarn. Each piece should be 18 in. long. Weave the yarn through the holes in the basket. Glue the ribbon on top for a handle. fill the basket with flowers.

**Error Summary**

| | |
|---|---|
| Capitalization | 2 |
| Punctuation: | |
| Comma | 1 |
| Period | 4 |

**TUESDAY**                                        **WEEK 18**

                    EMC 2725 • Daily Paragraph Editing, Grade 2 • ©2004 by Evan-Moor Corp.

Name _____

# Holiday Gifts

You can make a flag. For a valentine's Day gift. You need 18 in. of fabric for the flag. You also need fabric scraps paint, and glue. First, make a design using paint and scraps Next, find a stick that is 3 ft long. roll the end of the flag around the stick and glue it in place

- abbreviations
- holidays

**MONDAY**                                    **WEEK 18**

To make a may Day basket, get a green plastic strawberry basket a ribbon that's 12 in long, and 8 pieces of yarn. Each piece should be 18 i.n long. Weave the yarn through the holes in the basket. Glue the ribbon on top for a handle fill the basket with flowers

- abbreviations
- holidays

**TUESDAY**                                    **WEEK 18**

Leaf pictures make great thanksgiving gifts. You need fall leaves, waxed paper, and newspaper. Place the leaves between ~~to~~ two pieces of waxed paper. Lay the newspaper over it. Have an adult press it with a hot iron. Make a frame using strips of paper 1 in. wide.

**Error Summary**

| | |
|---|---|
| Capitalization | 1 |
| Punctuation: | |
| Comma | 1 |
| Period | 3 |
| Spelling | 1 |

**WEDNESDAY                    WEEK 18**

For christmas or Hanukkah, give a coupon book. Use 6 pieces of paper for the coupons and 2 pieces of colored paper. For the cover. Each coupon can be 2 in. wide by 5 in. long. staple the pages together. On each page, write a note like, "This coupon is good for ~~won~~ one hug."

**Error Summary**

| | |
|---|---|
| Capitalization | 3 |
| Punctuation: | |
| Period | 5 |
| Spelling | 1 |

**THURSDAY                    WEEK 18**

EMC 2725 • Daily Paragraph Editing, Grade 2 • ©2004 by Evan-Moor Corp.

Name _____

Leaf pictures make great thanksgiving gifts You need fall leaves waxed paper, and newspaper. Place the leaves between to pieces of waxed paper. Lay the newspaper over it Have an adult press it with a hot iron. Make a frame using strips of paper 1 i.n wide.

- abbreviations
- holidays

**WEDNESDAY**                                    **WEEK 18**

For christmas or Hanukkah, give a coupon book. Use 6 pieces of paper for the coupons and 2 pieces of colored paper. For the cover. Each coupon can be 2 in wide by 5 in long. staple the pages together On each page, write a note like, "This coupon is good for won hug"

- abbreviations
- holidays

**THURSDAY**                                    **WEEK 18**

Preview the 4 daily lessons to ensure you review or introduce skills that may be unfamiliar to students.

# My New Sister

sunday december 19 2004

Dear Diary,

　My new baby sister should be coming any day now? Dr. miller told Mom that she would come this week. I think she ~~wood~~ would make a great christmas present!

| Error Summary | |
|---|---|
| Capitalization | 4 |
| Punctuation: | |
| Comma | 3 |
| Period | 2 |
| Spelling | 1 |

**MONDAY**　　　　　　　　**WEEK 19**

　I can't wait to meet my new sister. I want to ~~teech~~ teach her new things. I hope she likes to read. Ill read her my favorite book. It's called I love you, Too.

　Yours truly,

　tim

| Error Summary | |
|---|---|
| Capitalization | 3 |
| Punctuation: | |
| Apostrophe | 2 |
| Comma | 1 |
| Other | 1 |
| Spelling | 1 |

**TUESDAY**　　　　　　　　**WEEK 19**

# My New Sister

sunday december 19 2004

Dear Diary

    My new baby sister should be coming any day now? Dr miller told Mom that she would come this week. I think she wood make a great christmas present!

- dates and greetings in letters
- names of people and holidays

**MONDAY**                                                **WEEK 19**

    I cant wait to meet my new sister. I want to teech her new things. I hope she likes to read. Ill read her my favorite book. It's called I love you, Too.

    Yours truly

    tim

- apostrophes
- closings in letters
- titles of books

**TUESDAY**                                             **WEEK 19**

friday, december 24, 2004

Dear Diary,

    Little emma was born at 1130 this morning! It's so exciting that she came on christmas eve. Dr. miller said that she's a beautiful baby. He's right!

**WEDNESDAY**                                    **WEEK 19**

| Error Summary | |
|---|---|
| Capitalization | 6 |
| Punctuation: | |
| Apostrophe | 3 |
| Comma | 3 |
| Period | 1 |
| Other | 2 |
| Spelling | 1 |

    I wrote emma a letter today. This is what I said:

Dear emma,

    Welcome to the world! I'm so glad you're here!

    Love,

    Your big brother tim

| Error Summary | |
|---|---|
| Capitalization | 3 |
| Punctuation: | |
| Apostrophe | 1 |
| Comma | 2 |
| Other | 1 |
| Spelling | 1 |

**THURSDAY**                                    **WEEK 19**

Name _____

friday december 24 2004

Dear Diary

　　Little emma was born at 1130 this morning! Its so exciting that she came on christmas eve. Dr miller said that shes a beautiful babee. Hes right

WATCH FOR

- apostrophes
- dates and greetings in letters
- names of people and holidays

**WEDNESDAY**　　　　　　　　　　　　**WEEK 19**

　　I wrote emma a letter today. This is what I said:

Dear emma

　　Welcome to the world! Im so glad your here

　　Love

　　Your big brother tim

WATCH FOR

- apostrophes
- greetings and closings in letters
- exclamation points

**THURSDAY**　　　　　　　　　　　　**WEEK 19**

Preview the 4 daily lessons to ensure you review or introduce skills that may be unfamiliar to students.

# Benjamin's Questions

How does that work? why does it do that? benjamin franklin asked questions like these. He was a very smart man who lived long ago. He did many tests. One of mr. franklin's tests was with a kite. It helped him learn about electricity. Have you ~~herd~~ heard about it?

| Error Summary | |
|---|---|
| Capitalization | 5 |
| Punctuation: | |
| Apostrophe | 1 |
| Period | 2 |
| Other | 3 |
| Spelling | 1 |

**MONDAY**　　　　　**WEEK 20**

benjamin franklin made a kite. He tied a key near the end of the kites string. ~~She~~ He hooked a wire to the key. mr. franklin flew the kite in a storm. Lightning hit the kite and went down the string. It hit the ~~kee~~ key and made a spark. This showed that lightning is electricity.

| Error Summary | |
|---|---|
| Capitalization | 4 |
| Language Usage | 1 |
| Punctuation: | |
| Apostrophe | 1 |
| Period | 2 |
| Spelling | 1 |

**TUESDAY**　　　　　**WEEK 20**

EMC 2725 • *Daily Paragraph Editing, Grade 2* • ©2004 by Evan-Moor Corp.

Name _____

# Benjamin's Questions

How does that work why does it do that benjamin franklin asked questions like these. He was a very smart man who lived long ago. He did many tests One of mr franklins tests was with a kite. It helped him learn about electricity. Have you herd about it.

WATCH FOR
- names of people
- question marks

| MONDAY | WEEK 20 |
|---|---|

benjamin franklin made a kite. He tied a key near the end of the kites string. She hooked a wire to the key. mr franklin flew the kite in a storm. Lightning hit the kite and went down the string. It hit the kee and made a spark. This showed that lightning is electricity

WATCH FOR
- names of people

| TUESDAY | WEEK 20 |
|---|---|

Mr. franklin used what he learned from his kite test. He put a metal rod on his house. In a storm, lightning hit the rod. it did not hitt [hit] the house. mr. franklins rod kept the house safe from lightning. Have you see [seen] lightning rods on houses these days.?

| Error Summary | |
| --- | --- |
| Capitalization | 4 |
| Language Usage | 1 |
| Punctuation: | |
| Apostrophe | 1 |
| Period | 2 |
| Other | 1 |
| Spelling | 1 |

**WEDNESDAY**                                    **WEEK 20**

Mr. franklin made many other things. Have you heard of a Franklin stove.? Its a special stove Mr. franklin made to heat peoples homes. Mr. Franklin also started the first fire company. She [He] wanted to help keep people safe from firs. [fires] Mr. franklin had many good ideas.

| Error Summary | |
| --- | --- |
| Capitalization | 3 |
| Language Usage | 1 |
| Punctuation: | |
| Apostrophe | 2 |
| Period | 4 |
| Other | 1 |
| Spelling | 1 |

**THURSDAY**                                    **WEEK 20**

Mr franklin used what he learned from his kite test. He put a metal rod on his house. In a storm, lightning hit the rod. it did not hitt the house. mr franklins rod kept the house safe from lightning. Have you see lightning rods on houses these days.

WATCH FOR

- names of people
- question marks

**WEDNESDAY**          **WEEK 20**

Mr franklin made many other things Have you heard of a Franklin stove. Its a special stove Mr franklin made to heat peoples homes. Mr. Franklin also started the first fire company. She wanted to help keep people safe from firs. Mr franklin had many good ideas.

WATCH FOR

- names of people
- question marks

**THURSDAY**          **WEEK 20**

Preview the 4 daily lessons to ensure you review or introduce skills that may be unfamiliar to students.

# Sun and Wind

Sun and Wind we're having an argument. Each claimed to be stronger just then, they saw a man strolling down a dusty road. "Let's see which of us can make the man take off his coat, said wind. "Then we will see who is stronger.

| Error Summary | |
|---|---|
| Capitalization | 2 |
| Punctuation: | |
|    Period | 1 |
|    Quotation Mark | 2 |
| Spelling | 1 |

**MONDAY**            **WEEK 21**

---

Wind went first. "I'll blow his coat off he said. He began to blow as hard as he could. The man buttoned his coat. Wind ~~blue~~ blew harder and harder. The harder he blew, the tighter the man held on to his coat Wind said, I give up.

| Error Summary | |
|---|---|
| Punctuation: | |
|    Apostrophe | 1 |
|    Comma | 1 |
|    Period | 1 |
|    Quotation Mark | 3 |
| Spelling | 1 |

**TUESDAY**            **WEEK 21**

EMC 2725 • Daily Paragraph Editing, Grade 2 • ©2004 by Evan-Moor Corp.

Name _____

# Sun and Wind

• dialog

Sun and Wind we're having an argument.
Each claimed to be stronger just then,
they saw a man strolling down a dusty road.
"Let's see which of us can make the man take
off his coat, said wind. "Then we will see who
is stronger.

**MONDAY**                                        **WEEK 21**

Wind went first. "Ill blow his coat off
he said. He began to blow as hard as he could.
The man buttoned his coat. Wind blue harder
and harder. The harder he blew, the tighter
the man held on to his coat Wind said, I
give up.

• dialog

**TUESDAY**                                       **WEEK 21**

Now it was Sun's turn. Sun beamed down on the man. Soon the man unbuttoned his coat. Sun began to shine even more brightly. the man soon found it too hot to walk. He stopped and pulled off his coat. he sat down on a large boulder under a shade tree to cool off.

**Error Summary**

| | |
|---|---|
| Capitalization | 2 |
| Punctuation: | |
| 　Apostrophe | 1 |
| 　Period | 3 |
| Spelling | 1 |

**WEDNESDAY**　　　　　　　　**WEEK 21**

In only a few minutes, Sun had won the contest. Wind asked, "how did you do that? You are no stronger than I am."

Sun replied, "you don't always need to use force to win."

**Error Summary**

| | |
|---|---|
| Capitalization | 2 |
| Punctuation: | |
| 　Period | 1 |
| 　Quotation Mark | 2 |
| 　Other | 1 |
| Spelling | 1 |

**THURSDAY**　　　　　　　　**WEEK 21**

Name _____

Now it was Suns turn Sun beamed down on the man. Soon the man unbuttoned his coat Sun began to shine even more brightly. the man soon found it too hot two walk. He stopped and pulled off his coat he sat down on a large boulder under a shade tree to cool off.

**WEDNESDAY**                                            **WEEK 21**

In only a few minutes, Sun had one the contest Wind asked, "how did you do that. You are no stronger than I am.

Sun replied, you don't always need to use force to win."

- dialog
- question marks

**THURSDAY**                                            **WEEK 21**

Preview the 4 daily lessons to ensure you review or introduce skills that may be unfamiliar to students.

# Trading Recipes

I have ~~to~~ <sup>two</sup> grandmothers. Granny is from norway. Mama Lupe is from New mexico. They like to ~~cooke~~ <sup>cook</sup>. one day, they decided to trade recipes. granny makes a ~~bred~~ <sup>bread</sup> called "lefse." Many people eat it in norway. She wrote her recipe for Mama Lupe on a recipe card⊙

| Error Summary | |
|---|---|
| Capitalization | 5 |
| Punctuation: | |
|   Period | 1 |
| Spelling | 3 |

**MONDAY**            **WEEK 22**

## LEFSE

Use 2 lbs. cooked potatoes, 1/2 c. butter, 1/2 c⊙cream, 1 Tbsp. sugar, 1 tsp. salt, and 2 1/2 c⊙flour.

Mash the potatoes with the butter⌄cream⌄sugar⌄and salt. Mix in the flour⊙roll the dough flat. cook it on a griddle. Flip the lefse and cook the other side. Yum!

| Error Summary | |
|---|---|
| Capitalization | 2 |
| Punctuation: | |
|   Comma | 3 |
|   Period | 3 |
|   Other | 1 |

Name _____

# Trading Recipes

I have to grandmothers. Granny is from norway. Mama Lupe is from New mexico. They like to cooke. one day, they decided to trade recipes. granny makes a bred called "lefse." Many people eat it in norway. She wrote her recipe for Mama Lupe on a recipe card

WATCH FOR

• names of places

---

**MONDAY**       **WEEK 22**

---

### LEFSE

Use 2 lbs. cooked potatoes, 1/2 c. butter, 1/2 c cream, 1 Tbsp. sugar, 1 tsp. salt, and 2 1/2 c flour.

Mash the potatoes with the butter cream sugar and salt. Mix in the flour roll the dough flat. cook it on a griddle. Flip the lefse and cook the other side. Yum

WATCH FOR

• abbreviations
• exclamation points

---

**TUESDAY**       **WEEK 22**

---

Mama lupe makes another kind of ~~bred~~ bread called "sopaipillas." They are from new mexico. mama Lupe sometimes serves them as dessert with honey or cinnamon sugar. That is my favorite way to ~~eet~~ eat them. Mama lupe wrote her sopaipilla recipe for Granny⊙

**Error Summary**

| | |
|---|---|
| Capitalization | 5 |
| Punctuation: | |
| Period | 1 |
| Spelling | 2 |

**WEDNESDAY**                    **WEEK 22**

## SOPAIPILLAS

Use 4 c⊙ flour, 1 Tbsp. baking powder, 2 Tbsp⊙ shortening, 1 tsp. salt, 3/4 c⊙ warm water, and oil for frying⊙

Mix the flour∧ baking powder∧ shortening, and salt together. Add the water⊙ heat the oil in a pan. Roll the dough and cut it into squares. ~~Fri~~ Fry the squares in hot oil. Enjoy!∧

**Error Summary**

| | |
|---|---|
| Capitalization | 1 |
| Punctuation: | |
| Comma | 2 |
| Period | 5 |
| Other | 1 |
| Spelling | 1 |

**THURSDAY**                    **WEEK 22**

Mama lupe makes another kind of bred called "sopaipillas." They are from new mexico. mama Lupe sometimes serves them as dessert with honey or cinnamon sugar. That is my favorite way to eet them. Mama lupe wrote her sopaipilla recipe for Granny

WATCH FOR

- names of people and places
- question marks

**WEDNESDAY**                                **WEEK 22**

## SOPAIPILLAS

Use 4 c flour, 1 Tbsp. baking powder, 2 Tbsp shortening, 1 tsp. salt, 3/4 c warm water, and oil for frying

Mix the flour baking powder shortening, and salt together. Add the water heat the oil in a pan. Roll the dough and cut it into squares. Fri the squares in hot oil. Enjoy

WATCH FOR

- abbreviations
- exclamation points

**THURSDAY**                                **WEEK 22**

Preview the 4 daily lessons to ensure you review or introduce skills that may be unfamiliar to students.

# Mr. Big's New Shoe

may 3, 1741, was a sunny day in the farm country of new york. Even so, danny smith was not happy. he had a problem. Although he was only seven, danny had many chores. One chore was to ~~chek~~ *check* the corn. He was riding out to the field when his pony, mr. Big, ~~begin~~ *began* to limp.

| Error Summary | |
|---|---|
| Capitalization | 7 |
| Language Usage | 1 |
| Punctuation: | |
|   Comma | 1 |
|   Period | 1 |
| Spelling | 1 |

**MONDAY**          **WEEK 23**

---

danny hopped off Mr. Big to see what was wrong. MR. Big lifted his foot. He seemed to say, "my foot is tender." danny saw that mr. big had lost a horseshoe. Danny walked the ~~ponie~~ *pony* back home. He told his Mother about the missing horseshoe.

| Error Summary | |
|---|---|
| Capitalization | 7 |
| Punctuation: | |
|   Comma | 1 |
|   Period | 3 |
|   Quotation Mark | 1 |
| Spelling | 1 |

**TUESDAY**          **WEEK 23**

# Mr. Big's New Shoe

may 3 1741, was a sunny day in the farm country of new york. Even so, danny smith was not happy. he had a problem. Although he was only seven, danny had many chores. One chore was to chek the corn He was riding out to the field when his pony, mr. Big, begin to limp.

- names of people, pets, and places

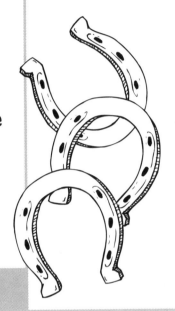

**MONDAY** **WEEK 23**

danny hopped off Mr Big to see what was wrong. MR Big lifted his foot. He seemed to say "my foot is tender. danny saw that m.r big had lost a horseshoe. Danny walked the ponie back home. He told his Mother about the missing horseshoe.

- names of people and pets
- abbreviations
- quotes

**TUESDAY** **WEEK 23**

Danny's mother told him he would have to go into town to see dr. Taylor at the blacksmith shop. "take polly," said Mother. Danny found his sister washing the clothes. She was glad to take a ~~brake~~ break from the hard work. Danny, Polly, and mr. Big went to dr. Taylor's shop.

### Error Summary

| | |
|---|---|
| Capitalization | 5 |
| Punctuation: | |
|    Apostrophe | 2 |
|    Period | 2 |
|    Quotation Mark | 1 |
| Spelling | 1 |

**WEDNESDAY**                    **WEEK 23**

Watching dr. taylor work was amazing! He took a ~~peece~~ piece of iron from the fire. It was so hot that it bent easily when Dr. taylor pounded it. He curved it into a horseshoe. He put it on Mr. Big's hoof. Mr. big whinnied as if to say, "Thanks for my new shoe!"

### Error Summary

| | |
|---|---|
| Capitalization | 4 |
| Punctuation: | |
|    Period | 4 |
|    Quotation Mark | 1 |
| Spelling | 1 |

**THURSDAY**                    **WEEK 23**

Name _____

Dannys mother told him he would have to go into town to see dr Taylor at the blacksmith shop. "take polly, said Mother. Danny found his sister washing the clothes. She was glad to take a brake from the hard work. Danny, Polly, and mr Big went to dr. Taylors shop.

- names of people and pets
- abbreviations
- dialog

**WEDNESDAY**                                    **WEEK 23**

Watching dr. taylor work was amazing! He took a peece of iron from the fire. It was so hot that it bent easily when Dr taylor pounded it. He curved it into a horseshoe He put it on Mr Big's hoof. Mr big whinnied as if to say, "Thanks for my new shoe!

- names of people and pets
- abbreviations
- dialog

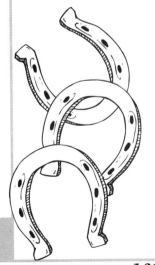

**THURSDAY**                                    **WEEK 23**

Preview the 4 daily lessons to ensure you review or introduce skills that may be unfamiliar to students.

# A Lot of Water

have you ever been to a lake? What did you do when you were ~~their~~ there? Did you look out at trees on the other side of the lake? think about looking across a lake and seeing only water. Thats what you would see if you we're looking at one of the five Great Lakes.

**Error Summary**

| | |
|---|---|
| Capitalization | 2 |
| Punctuation: | |
| Apostrophe | 1 |
| Other | 2 |
| Spelling | 2 |

**MONDAY**                                    **WEEK 24**

The Great Lakes are named Superior, michigan Huron, Erie, and Ontario. On a map, lake superior looks like a wolfs head. Lakes Michigan huron, and Erie form the outline of a mitten. lake Michigan is only in the United states. The other lakes are also in canada.

**Error Summary**

| | |
|---|---|
| Capitalization | 7 |
| Punctuation: | |
| Apostrophe | 1 |
| Comma | 3 |

**TUESDAY**                                   **WEEK 24**

# A Lot of Water

• question marks

have you ever been to a lake. What did you do when you were their? Did you look out at trees on the other side of the lake. think about looking across a lake and seeing only water. Thats what you would see if you we're looking at one of the five Great Lakes.

**MONDAY**                                          **WEEK 24**

---

The Great Lakes are named Superior michigan Huron, Erie, and Ontario. On a map, lake superior looks like a wolfs head. Lakes Michigan huron, and Erie form the outline of a mitten. lake Michigan is only in the United states. The other lakes are also in canada.

• names of places
• commas

**TUESDAY**                                          **WEEK 24**

The great Lakes are the largest group of freshwater lakes in the world. They hold millions of gallons of water. What if you could stretch the lakes from one end of the United states to the other? the water would be about 108 inches (9 ft) deep?

**Error Summary**

| | |
|---|---|
| Capitalization | 3 |
| Punctuation: | |
| Period | 3 |
| Other | 1 |

**WEDNESDAY**                                   **WEEK 24**

The Great lakes are not all at the same height. lake erie is more than 106 yards (320 ft) higher than lake Ontario. the water falls from one lake to the other. The place where this happens is called Niagara falls. It is a famous, beautiful, and exciting place to visit!

**Error Summary**

| | |
|---|---|
| Capitalization | 6 |
| Punctuation: | |
| Period | 1 |

**THURSDAY**                                   **WEEK 24**

EMC 2725 • Daily Paragraph Editing, Grade 2 • ©2004 by Evan-Moor Corp.

Name _____

The great Lakes are the largest group of freshwater lakes in the world. They hold millions of gallons of water What if you could stretch the lakes from one end of the United states to the other. the water would be about 108 inches (9 ft) deep?

- names of places
- question marks

**WEDNESDAY**                    **WEEK 24**

The Great lakes are not all at the same height. lake erie is more than 106 yards (320 ft) higher than lake Ontario. the water falls from one lake to the other. The place where this happens is called Niagara falls. It is a famous, beautiful, and exciting place to visit!

- names of places
- abbreviations

**THURSDAY**                    **WEEK 24**

Preview the 4 daily lessons to ensure you review or introduce skills that may be unfamiliar to students.

# An Understanding Mom

"Ouch! I yelled as i fell off my bike again. Ill never learn how to ride without training wheels!"

Mom said, "I understand how you feel, tommy.

I yelled back, "you do not! I stormed into the house. That's when I saw the box on the table
~~tabel~~.

| Error Summary | |
|---|---|
| Capitalization | 3 |
| Punctuation: | |
|   Apostrophe | 2 |
|   Quotation Mark | 5 |
|   Other | 1 |
| Spelling | 1 |

**MONDAY**        **WEEK 25**

I opened the box and saw something that looked like a radio. i turned it on. Suddenly, I was in another place. The time on the wall clock was 6:15. "patricia, it's time for dinner," a woman called. A seven-year-old girl came in from outside. She was crying.

| Error Summary | |
|---|---|
| Capitalization | 2 |
| Punctuation: | |
|   Apostrophe | 1 |
|   Period | 2 |
|   Quotation Mark | 1 |
|   Other | 1 |

**TUESDAY**        **WEEK 25**

# An Understanding Mom

Ouch I yelled as i fell off my bike again. Ill never learn how to ride without training wheels!"

Mom said, "I understand how you feel, tommy.

I yelled back, "you do not! I stormed into the house. Thats when I saw the box on the tabel.

WATCH FOR

- dialog
- exclamation points

**MONDAY**                                        **WEEK 25**

---

I opened the box and saw something that looked like a radio i turned it on. Suddenly, I was in another place. The time on the wall clock was 6-15. "patricia, its time for dinner, a woman called. A seven-year-old girl came in from outside. She was crying

WATCH FOR

- dialog
- colons in time

**TUESDAY**                                        **WEEK 25**

The girl wailed, "mom, I'll never learn how to ride my bike! All the other kids can do it." The girl looked familiar. She looked like pat, my mom. I looked at the calendar on the ~~woll~~ wall. It read april 23, 1970. I had gone back in time! I was in my grandparents' old house!

**Error Summary**

| Capitalization | 3 |
|---|---|
| Punctuation: | |
| Apostrophe | 2 |
| Comma | 1 |
| Quotation Mark | 1 |
| Other | 1 |
| Spelling | 1 |

**WEDNESDAY**      **WEEK 25**

I turned the radio off and closed my eyes. When I opened them, i was back in my kitchen. The calendar had today's date, april 23, 2004. My mom hugged me and said, "there you are. It's 6:15 and time for dinner. Don't worry. You'll learn to ride soon. I did, and so can you."

**Error Summary**

| Capitalization | 3 |
|---|---|
| Punctuation: | |
| Apostrophe | 3 |
| Comma | 1 |
| Period | 1 |
| Other | 1 |

**THURSDAY**      **WEEK 25**

EMC 2725 • Daily Paragraph Editing, Grade 2 • ©2004 by Evan-Moor Corp.

The girl wailed, mom, Ill never learn how to ride my bike! All the other kids can do it." The girl looked familiar. She looked like pat, my mom. I looked at the calendar on the woll. It read april 23 1970. I had gone back in time I was in my grandparents old house!

WATCH FOR

- dialog
- dates
- colons in time

**WEDNESDAY**                    **WEEK 25**

I turned the radio off and closed my eyes. When I opened them, i was back in my kitchen. The calendar had today's date, april 23 2004. My mom hugged me and said, "there you are. Its 615 and time for dinner. Dont worry. Youll learn to ride soon. I did, and so can you"

WATCH FOR

- dialog
- dates
- colons in time

**THURSDAY**                    **WEEK 25**

Preview the 4 daily lessons to ensure you review or introduce skills that may be unfamiliar to students.

# My Field Trip Journal

wednesday, march 10, 2004

Dear Diary,

   We made it? My class is here in

Kayenta, arizona. We came to learn about

the Navajo people. It took ~~too~~ two days to

get here. we are glad to be off the bus

at last.

| Error Summary | |
|---|---|
| Capitalization | 4 |
| Punctuation: | |
| Comma | 4 |
| Period | 2 |
| Spelling | 1 |

**MONDAY**                    **WEEK 26**

   After a rest, we went to the ~~skool~~ school in

kayenta. most of the students are Navajo.

In addition to the subjects I learn, they

also study the navajo language.

   Yours truly,

sara

| Error Summary | |
|---|---|
| Capitalization | 4 |
| Punctuation: | |
| Comma | 1 |
| Spelling | 1 |

**TUESDAY**                    **WEEK 26**

# My Field Trip Journal

wednesday march 10 2004

Dear Diary

    We made it? My class is here in Kayenta arizona We came to learn about the Navajo people. It took too days to get here. we are glad to be off the bus at last.

- dates and greetings in letters
- names of places

**MONDAY**                                          **WEEK 26**

---

    After a rest, we went to the skool in kayenta. most of the students are Navajo. In addition to the subjects I learn, they also study the navajo language.

    Yours truly

    sara

- closings in letters
- names of places, groups of people, and languages

**TUESDAY**                                          **WEEK 26**

friday, march, 12, 2004

Dear Diary,

It is our last day in kayenta, arizona. We go back home by bus on saturaday. [Saturday] Last night, we went to a Navajo powwow. We all danced to the beet [beat] of the dums [drums].

**Error Summary**

| Capitalization | 5 |
| Punctuation: | |
| Comma | 5 |
| Period | 1 |
| Spelling | 3 |

**WEDNESDAY** **WEEK 26**

We saw a traditional Navajo home. It's called a "hogan." It's made with logs, bushes, and mud. it has six or eight sides and a rownd [round] roof. The door faces east.

yours truly,

sara

**Error Summary**

| Capitalization | 3 |
| Punctuation: | |
| Apostrophe | 2 |
| Comma | 3 |
| Period | 2 |
| Spelling | 1 |

**THURSDAY** **WEEK 26**

EMC 2725 • Daily Paragraph Editing, Grade 2 • ©2004 by Evan-Moor Corp.

friday march, 12 2004

Dear Diary

    It is our last day in kayenta arizona. We go back home by bus on saturaday. Last night, we went to a Navajo powwow We all danced to the beet of the dums.

WATCH FOR

- dates and greetings in letters
- names of places and days of the week

**WEDNESDAY**　　　　　　　　　　**WEEK 26**

---

    We saw a traditional Navajo home Its called a "hogan." Its made with logs bushes and mud. it has six or eight sides and a rownd roof. The door faces east

    yours truly

    sara

WATCH FOR

- closings in letters

**THURSDAY**　　　　　　　　　　**WEEK 26**

Preview the 4 daily lessons to ensure you review or introduce skills that may be unfamiliar to students.

# Meet Michelle Lee

Michelle lee (ML) is an author. She was interviewed by a writer for Kids' history (KH) magazine.

KH: You did a great job on your latest book, michelle. Kids everywhere are ~~reeding~~ reading it.

ML: Thanks! Im very proud of A Walk Through Time.

**Error Summary**

| | |
|---|---|
| Capitalization | 3 |
| Punctuation: | |
|    Apostrophe | 1 |
|    Other | 1 |
| Spelling | 1 |

**MONDAY**          **WEEK 27**

---

KH: Your new book, a walk Through Time, is about American history. Why are you interested in history.?

ML: I was born on february 22, 1965. Many years before, george washington was born on that same day. Ive always been interested in this great man.

**Error Summary**

| | |
|---|---|
| Capitalization | 5 |
| Punctuation: | |
|    Apostrophe | 1 |
|    Comma | 1 |
|    Other | 1 |

**TUESDAY**          **WEEK 27**

Name _____

# Meet Michelle Lee

Michelle lee (ML) is an author. She was interviewed by a writer for <u>Kids' history</u> (KH) magazine.

KH: You did a great job on your latest book, michelle. Kids everywhere are reeding it.

ML: Thanks! Im very proud of A Walk Through Time.

• names of people, magazines, and books

**MONDAY**                                    **WEEK 27**

---

KH: Your new book, <u>a walk Through Time</u>, is about American history. Why are you interested in history.

ML: I was born on february 22 1965. Many years before, george washington was born on that same day. Ive always been interested in this great man.

• names of people and books
• question marks
• dates

**TUESDAY**                                    **WEEK 27**

**KH:** Does Presidents' Day have special meaning for you.?

**ML:** Yes, it does? Many people only think about valentine's day in february. But for me, the best holiday is presidents' day. Our country has had many great leaders. Their stories are amazing!

| Error Summary | |
| --- | --- |
| Capitalization | 5 |
| Punctuation: | |
| Period | 2 |
| Other | 1 |

**WEDNESDAY**      **WEEK 27**

**KH:** Your book isnt like other history books. Its a lot of fun to read your stories about the presidents.

**ML:** Some kids think history is boring. Its important for them to see that history can be exciting. My book, a walk Through time, has fun stories from history.

| Error Summary | |
| --- | --- |
| Capitalization | 3 |
| Punctuation: | |
| Apostrophe | 3 |
| Period | 2 |
| Other | 1 |

**THURSDAY**      **WEEK 27**

EMC 2725 • Daily Paragraph Editing, Grade 2 • ©2004 by Evan-Moor Corp.

KH: Does Presidents' Day have special meaning for you.

ML: Yes, it does? Many people only think about valentine's day in february. But for me, the best holiday is presidents' day. Our country has had many great leaders Their stories are amazing!

• names of holidays and months

**WEDNESDAY**                    **WEEK 27**

KH: Your book isnt like other history books. Its a lot of fun to read your stories about the presidents

ML: Some kids think history is boring. Its important for them to see that history can be exciting. My book, a walk Through time, has fun stories from history

• names of books

**THURSDAY**                    **WEEK 27**

Preview the 4 daily lessons to ensure you review or introduce skills that may be unfamiliar to students.

# A Long Trip Home

On april 5, 1882, my family began to travel west. Pa brought a ~~knew~~ new covered wagon to our house. We loaded it with food, tools, and a trunk. The rest had to stay behind. Pa hitched the horses to the wagon. I waved and said, "So long, St. louis, Missouri."

**Error Summary**

| | |
|---|---|
| Capitalization | 2 |
| Punctuation: | |
| Comma | 4 |
| Period | 2 |
| Spelling | 1 |

**MONDAY**                          **WEEK 28**

---

It was not an easy trip. We rode in the wagon all day. We slept in it at night. the food was terrible. I missed home. Finally, we met up with other families. We were all going to portland, oregon. I ~~hopped~~ hoped that the trip would be better now.

**Error Summary**

| | |
|---|---|
| Capitalization | 3 |
| Punctuation: | |
| Comma | 1 |
| Period | 3 |
| Spelling | 1 |

**TUESDAY**                          **WEEK 28**

EMC 2725 • Daily Paragraph Editing, Grade 2 • ©2004 by Evan-Moor Corp.

Name

# A Long Trip Home

On april 5 1882, my family began to travel west Pa brought a knew covered wagon to our house. We loaded it with food tools and a trunk. The rest had to stay behind Pa hitched the horses to the wagon. I waved and said, "So long, St. louis Missouri."

WATCH FOR
- commas
- names of places

| MONDAY | WEEK 28 |
|---|---|

It was not an easy trip. We rode in the wagon all day We slept in it at night the food was terrible. I missed home. Finally, we met up with other families. We were all going to portland oregon. I hopped that the trip would be better now

WATCH FOR
- commas
- names of places

| TUESDAY | WEEK 28 |
|---|---|

I was wrong. The trip was long and hard, even with the 100 wagons ~~moveing~~ moving together. It was really hot. it rained so much once that our wheels stuck in the mud. Many men worked to pull us out and fix the wheels. But the worst part was when many of us got sick.

**WEDNESDAY**                    **WEEK 28**

We arrived in portland, Oregon, on september 16, 1882. We traveled more than 3,000 kilometers. In those five months. At first, I missed my home in St. louis. Now, I happily call portland my home. I also have many ~~storys~~ stories to tell about my trip here.

**ETHURSDAY**                    **WEEK 28**

I was wrong. The trip was long and hard, even with the 100 wagons moveing together. It was really hot it rained so much once that our wheels stuck in the mud. Many men worked to pull us out and fix the wheels But the worst part was when many of us got sick

WEDNESDAY                                        WEEK 28

We arrived in portland Oregon, on september 16 1882. We traveled more than 3,000 kilometers. In those five months. At first, I missed my home in St. louis. Now, I happily call portland my home. I also have many storys to tell about my trip here

WATCH FOR

• commas
• names of places

THURSDAY                                        WEEK 28

Preview the 4 daily lessons to ensure you review or introduce skills that may be unfamiliar to students.

# A Telescope in the Sky

I bet you know that the moon goes around Earth. There's something else in the sky that also goes around Earth. It is a huge telescope. a telescope makes things that are far away look ~~near~~ near. People use telescopes, To learn about things in space.

**Error Summary**

Capitalization 2
Punctuation:
 Apostrophe 1
 Period 3
Spelling 1

**MONDAY**                     **WEEK 29**

On april 25, 1990, people flew into space on a space shuttle. They took the Hubble Space Telescope with them. they took the telescope ~~owt~~ out of the shuttle. They put it out in space. it began to go around Earth. Then the people came back to Earth?

**Error Summary**

Capitalization 3
Punctuation:
 Comma 1
 Period 3
Spelling 1

**TUESDAY**                    **WEEK 29**

# A Telescope in the Sky

I bet you know that the moon goes around Earth. Theres something else in the sky that also goes around Earth. It is a huge telescope a telescope makes things that are far away look neer. People use telescopes. To learn about things in space

**MONDAY**                                        **WEEK 29**

On april 25 1990, people flew into space on a space shuttle. They took the Hubble Space Telescope with them they took the telescope owt of the shuttle. They put it out in space it began to go around Earth. Then the people came back to Earth?

WATCH FOR

• dates

**TUESDAY**                                        **WEEK 29**

The Hubble Space Telescope is still in
space
spase it is about 610 kilometers (380 mi) above
us. You know that the moon circles Earth about
month
once a munth. Hubble makes a circle around
Earth about once, Every hour and a half! It
travels 444 kilometers (276 mi) each minute.

**Error Summary**

| | |
|---|---|
| Capitalization | 2 |
| Punctuation: | |
| Period | 5 |
| Spelling | 2 |

**WEDNESDAY**                                        **WEEK 29**

We have learned a lot about space from
the Hubble Space Telescope it has taken
pictures of things that are far from Earth.
On february 21 1994, Hubble took a picture
of the planet Pluto we learned that it is
2,320 kilometers (1,440 mi) wide.

**Error Summary**

| | |
|---|---|
| Capitalization | 3 |
| Punctuation: | |
| Comma | 1 |
| Period | 3 |

**THURSDAY**                                         **WEEK 29**

The Hubble Space Telescope is still in spase it is about 610 kilometers (380 mi) above us. You know that the moon circles Earth about once a munth. Hubble makes a circle around Earth about once. Every hour and a half! It travels 444 kilometers (276 mi) each minute

WATCH FOR

• abbreviations

**WEDNESDAY**                                    **WEEK 29**

We have learned a lot about space from the Hubble Space Telescope it has taken pictures of things that are far from Earth. On february 21 1994, Hubble took a picture of the planet Pluto we learned that it is 2,320 kilometers (1,440 mi) wide.

WATCH FOR

• abbreviations
• dates

**THURSDAY**                                     **WEEK 29**

Preview the 4 daily lessons to ensure you review or introduce skills that may be unfamiliar to students.

# Tell All About It

do you have a classroom pet or a pet at home? How would you tell someone about it? you might tell what it looks like. You could say, "it is red. It has two wings and feathers." The other person would know your pet was a ~~burd~~ bird. But there is more you could say.

| Error Summary | |
|---|---|
| Capitalization | 3 |
| Punctuation: | |
| Period | 1 |
| Quotation Mark | 1 |
| Other | 2 |
| Spelling | 1 |

**MONDAY**                                        **WEEK 30**

---

All things can be described. when you tell about something, you might tell about it's properties. you can tell about something's color, size, weight, and shape. Tools help you measure these properties. You need to know when to use the different tools.

| Error Summary | |
|---|---|
| Capitalization | 2 |
| Punctuation: | |
| Apostrophe | 1 |
| Comma | 2 |
| Period | 3 |

**TUESDAY**                                        **WEEK 30**

EMC 2725 • Daily Paragraph Editing, Grade 2 • ©2004 by Evan-Moor Corp.

# Tell All About It

- question marks
- quotes

do you have a classroom pet or a pet at home How would you tell someone about it. you might tell what it looks like. You could say, "it is red. It has two wings and feathers. The other person would know your pet was a burd. But there is more you could say

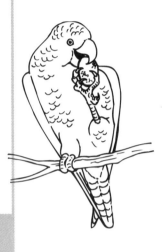

**MONDAY**                                    **WEEK 30**

All things can be described. when you tell about something, you might tell about it's properties you can tell about something's color size weight, and shape. Tools help you measure these properties You need to know when to use the different tools

- commas

**TUESDAY**                                    **WEEK 30**

think about the pet bird. You described its color. How would you learn about its size? You could use a ruler. a small bird might be 8 centimeters (3 in) tall. A larger bird, such as a parrot, might be 61 centimeters (24 in) tall. What else could you tell about your bird.?

**Error Summary**

| Capitalization | 2 |
|---|---|
| Punctuation: | |
| Period | 4 |
| Other | 2 |

**WEDNESDAY**                                    **WEEK 30**

Use a scale to learn how much your bird weighs. the small bird might ~~way~~ weigh 85 grams (3 oz). the bigger bird might weigh 2 kilograms (4 lb). That is the same as 2,000 grams (70.5 oz). When you tell about something, think about all of it's properties.

**Error Summary**

| Capitalization | 2 |
|---|---|
| Punctuation: | |
| Apostrophe | 1 |
| Period | 4 |
| Spelling | 1 |

**THURSDAY**                                    **WEEK 30**

think about the pet bird You described its color. How would you learn about its size. You could use a ruler a small bird might be 8 centimeters (3 .in) tall. A larger bird, such as a parrot, might be 61 centimeters (24 in) tall. What else could you tell about your bird.

- question marks
- abbreviations

**WEDNESDAY**                                    **WEEK 30**

Use a scale to learn how much your bird weighs the small bird might way 85 grams (3 o.z). the bigger bird might weigh 2 kilograms (4 .lb). That is the same as 2,000 grams (70.5 oz). When you tell about something, think about all of it's properties.

- abbreviations

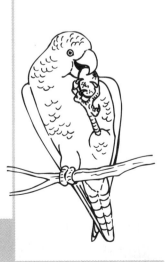

**THURSDAY**                                    **WEEK 30**

Preview the 4 daily lessons to ensure you review or introduce skills that may be unfamiliar to students.

# Sunlight on the Moon

The moon does not make it's own light. it reflects light from the sun? As the moon goes around Earth each month, different amounts of sunlight shine on it Thats why the moon can look different. Now, imagine it is november 2 2005. Tonight, you see no moon at all

**Error Summary**

| | |
|---|---|
| Capitalization | 2 |
| Punctuation: | |
| Apostrophe | 2 |
| Comma | 1 |
| Period | 3 |

**MONDAY**                                            **WEEK 31**

---

When the moon is between the sun and Earth, it looks dark the dark moon is called a "new moon." Each night, the moon moves a little by november 9 2005, some of the sun's light is shining on the moon The slice of moon that you can see sea now is called a "quarter moon."

**Error Summary**

| | |
|---|---|
| Capitalization | 3 |
| Punctuation: | |
| Comma | 1 |
| Period | 3 |
| Spelling | 1 |

**TUESDAY**                                           **WEEK 31**

# Sunlight on the Moon

The moon does not make it's own light. it reflects light from the sun? As the moon goes around Earth each month, different amounts of sunlight shine on it Thats why the moon can look different. Now, imagine it is november 2 2005. Tonight, you see no moon at all

• dates

**MONDAY**                                   **WEEK 31**

---

When the moon is between the sun and Earth, it looks dark the dark moon is called a "new moon." Each night, the moon moves a little by november 9 2005, some of the sun's light is shining on the moon The slice of moon that you can sea now is called a "quarter moon."

• dates

**TUESDAY**                                  **WEEK 31**

the sun's light shines on one full side of the moon on november 16, 2005. This is a "full moon". As the moon travels, less light shines on it. You see another quarter moon on november 23, 2005. The moon is dark again on december 1, 2005. It is another new moon.

**Error Summary**

| | |
|---|---|
| Capitalization | 4 |
| Punctuation: | |
| Apostrophe | 1 |
| Comma | 3 |
| Period | 3 |

**WEDNESDAY**　　　　　　　**WEEK 31**

When you see the second new moon, you know no the moon has circled Earth one time. The phases of the moon will start again. there are many books you can reed read to learn more about the moon. You might enjoy <u>The Moon Book</u> by gail gibbons.

**Error Summary**

| | |
|---|---|
| Capitalization | 3 |
| Punctuation: | |
| Period | 2 |
| Other | 1 |
| Spelling | 2 |

**THURSDAY**　　　　　　　**WEEK 31**

the suns light shines on one full side of the moon on november 16 2005. This is a "full moon" As the moon travels, less light shines on it. You see another quarter moon on november 23 2005. The moon is dark again on december 1 2005 It is another new moon

• dates

**WEDNESDAY**                                     **WEEK 31**

---

When you see the second new moon, you no the moon has circled Earth one time. The phases of the moon will start again there are many books you can reed to learn more about the moon You might enjoy The Moon Book by gail gibbons.

• titles of books

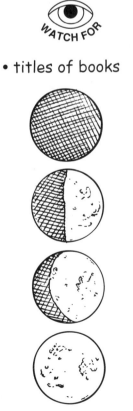

**THURSDAY**                                     **WEEK 31**

Preview the 4 daily lessons to ensure you review or introduce skills that may be unfamiliar to students.

# Niagara Falls

Niagara Falls is known around the world⊙ it is on the border of the united States and canada. The falls are about 1,000 meters (1,094 yd) across. That is longer than 10 football fields! Look at the falls⊙ ~~Here~~ Hear the roaring water. feel the cool mist on your skin.

| Error Summary | |
|---|---|
| Capitalization | 4 |
| Punctuation: | |
| Period | 3 |
| Spelling | 1 |

**MONDAY**                                    **WEEK 32**

The ~~fals~~ falls form a horseshoe shape. goat Island splits the falls into two parts. the larger part is Horseshoe falls. It is in canada. It is 670 meters (2,200 ft) from goat island to the shore. the water of horseshoe falls drops down 56 meters (185 ft)⊙

| Error Summary | |
|---|---|
| Capitalization | 9 |
| Punctuation: | |
| Period | 2 |
| Spelling | 1 |

**TUESDAY**                                    **WEEK 32**

Name —————————————————————————

# Niagara Falls

Niagara Falls is known around the world it is on the border of the united States and canada. The falls are about 1,000 meters (1,094 yd) across. That is longer than 10 football fields! Look at the falls Here the roaring water. feel the cool mist on your skin.

- abbreviations
- names of places

**MONDAY**          **WEEK 32**

The fals form a horseshoe shape. goat Island splits the falls into two parts. the larger part is Horseshoe falls. It is in canada. It is 670 meters (2,200 f.t) from goat island to the shore. the water of horseshoe falls drops down 56 meters (185 ft).

- abbreviations
- names of places

**TUESDAY**          **WEEK 32**

The American Falls are on the other side of goat island. These falls are about 320 meters (1,050 ft) across. That is the distance from the American shore to goat island. water from american falls drops down doun 58 meters (190 ft).

**Error Summary**

| Capitalization | 7 |
| Punctuation: | |
| Period | 2 |
| Spelling | 1 |

**WEDNESDAY**                                    **WEEK 32**

Walk across a bridge from the edge of american Falls to goat island. Ride an elevator to the bottom botem of the falls. stand behind a curtain of water. It is only one-half meter (25 ft) from you. feel the wind and the mist. This place is called the "Cave of the winds."

**Error Summary**

| Capitalization | 6 |
| Punctuation: | |
| Period | 1 |
| Spelling | 1 |

**ETHURSDAY**                                    **WEEK 32**

EMC 2725 • Daily Paragraph Editing, Grade 2 • ©2004 by Evan-Moor Corp.

The American Falls are on the other side of goat island. These falls are about 320 meters (1,050 ft) across. That is the distance from the American shore to goat island. water from american falls drops doun 58 meters (190 .ft).

- abbreviations
- names of places

**WEDNESDAY**                     **WEEK 32**

Walk across a bridge from the edge of american Falls to goat island. Ride an elevator to the botom of the falls. stand behind a curtain of water. It is only one-half meter (25 ft) from you. feel the wind and the mist. This place is called the "Cave of the winds."

- abbreviations
- names of places

**THURSDAY**                     **WEEK 32**

Preview the 4 daily lessons to ensure you review or introduce skills that may be unfamiliar to students.

# Country Mouse in the City

One sunny day, City Mouse ~~goed~~ *went* to visit his cousin in the country. city mouse didn't like country Mouse's straw beds or seed dinners. He asked country mouse, "How can you eat this food? How can you sleep on straw? Come to the city to see how i live."

| Error Summary | |
|---|---|
| Capitalization | 6 |
| Language Usage | 1 |
| Punctuation: | |
| Comma | 1 |
| Period | 1 |
| Quotation Mark | 1 |
| Other | 2 |

**MONDAY**　　　　　　　　**WEEK 33**

---

City mouse and country Mouse set off for the city. It was late when they came to the house where city Mouse lived. City mouse ~~showing~~ *showed* his cousin a nest of cotton rags. He said to country Mouse, "This is where we will sleep. But first, let's eat."

| Error Summary | |
|---|---|
| Capitalization | 5 |
| Language Usage | 1 |
| Punctuation: | |
| Apostrophe | 1 |
| Quotation Mark | 1 |

**TUESDAY**　　　　　　　　**WEEK 33**

# Country Mouse in the City

One sunny day, City Mouse goed to visit his cousin in the country city mouse didn't like country Mouse's straw beds or seed dinners. He asked country mouse "How can you eat this food. How can you sleep on straw. Come to the city to see how i live.

• dialog
• question marks

**MONDAY**                                **WEEK 33**

City mouse and country Mouse set off for the city. It was late when they came to the house where city Mouse lived. City mouse showing his cousin a nest of cotton rags. He said to country Mouse, This is where we will sleep. But first, lets eat."

• dialog

**TUESDAY**                                **WEEK 33**

city mouse led his cousin to the dining room. They were soon eating ~~bred~~ bread crusts, peas, and cake. City mouse asked, "do you like what i eat?" While they ate, danger was coming closer. Suddenly, they heard a loud snarl. "It's the cat!" City Mouse shouted.

**Error Summary**

| | |
|---|---|
| Capitalization | 5 |
| Punctuation: | |
| Apostrophe | 1 |
| Quotation Mark | 1 |
| Other | 1 |
| Spelling | 1 |

**WEDNESDAY**                                              **WEEK 33**

The cat jumped at the mice. They ran into a hole in the wall. country mouse packed his suitcase. city Mouse asked his cousin where he was going. Country Mouse said, "It's better to eat ~~seads~~ seeds in a safe place than to eat cake where there's a cat!" And off he went.

**Error Summary**

| | |
|---|---|
| Capitalization | 3 |
| Punctuation: | |
| Period | 3 |
| Quotation Mark | 1 |
| Spelling | 1 |

**THURSDAY**                                                **WEEK 33**

EMC 2725 • Daily Paragraph Editing, Grade 2 • ©2004 by Evan-Moor Corp.

Name _____

city mouse led his cousin to the dining room. They were soon eating bred crusts, peas, and cake. City mouse asked, "do you like what i eat. While they ate, danger was coming closer. Suddenly, they heard a loud snarl. "Its the cat!" City Mouse shouted.

WATCH FOR

- dialog
- question marks

**WEDNESDAY**      **WEEK 33**

The cat jumped at the mice They ran into a hole in the wall country mouse packed his suitcase. city Mouse asked his cousin where he was going? Country Mouse said, "It's better to eat seads in a safe place than to eat cake where there's a cat! And off he went.

WATCH FOR

- dialog

**THURSDAY**      **WEEK 33**

Preview the 4 daily lessons to ensure you review or introduce skills that may be unfamiliar to students.

# A Welcome

The word on the doormat says, "welcome." The person who opens the door says, "Come in. Have you ever been greeted with a warm welcome? People who arrive at new york Harbor get a special welcome. The Statue of Liberty welcomes them to the united states of america.

**Error Summary**

| | |
|---|---|
| Capitalization | 6 |
| Punctuation: | |
| Period | 1 |
| Quotation Mark | 1 |
| Other | 1 |

**MONDAY**       **WEEK 34**

---

The Statue of Liberty is a statue of a woman. She is tall (151 ft), and so is the base where she stands (154 ft). She holds a burning torch in one hand, And a tablet in the other. She has a crown on her ~~hed~~ head and a broken chain at her feet. She stands for freedom.

**Error Summary**

| | |
|---|---|
| Capitalization | 1 |
| Punctuation: | |
| Period | 5 |
| Spelling | 1 |

**TUESDAY**       **WEEK 34**

# A Welcome

The word on the doormat says, "welcome"
The person who opens the door says, "Come
in. Have you ever been greeted with a warm
welcome. People who arrive at new york Harbor
get a special welcome. The Statue of Liberty
welcomes them to the united states of america.

• names of places

**MONDAY**             **WEEK 34**

---

The Statue of Liberty is a statue of a
woman She is tall (151 ft), and so is the base
where she stands (154 ft). She holds a burning
torch in one hand. And a tablet in the other.
She has a crown on her hed and a broken
chain at her feet. She stands for freedom

• abbreviations

**TUESDAY**             **WEEK 34**

emma lazarus wrote a poem about the Statue of Liberty. You can ~~reed~~ read it on the base of the statue. part of it says, "Give me your tired, your poor...I lift my lamp beside the golden door!" The lamp that the statue lifts is a torch. the golden door is the united states.

## Error Summary

| | |
|---|---|
| Capitalization | 6 |
| Punctuation: | |
| Period | 1 |
| Quotation Mark | 1 |
| Spelling | 1 |

**WEDNESDAY**                    **WEEK 34**

If you go to new york, take a ferry ride out to Liberty Island. visit the Statue of Liberty. Read the poem. go inside the statue. Look out over new york Harbor. Think of all the ~~peeple~~ people who have said, "Thank you!" to the Statue of Liberty's welcome.

## Error Summary

| | |
|---|---|
| Capitalization | 6 |
| Punctuation: | |
| Apostrophe | 1 |
| Period | 2 |
| Quotation Mark | 1 |
| Spelling | 1 |

**THURSDAY**                    **WEEK 34**

EMC 2725 • Daily Paragraph Editing, Grade 2 • ©2004 by Evan-Moor Corp.

emma lazarus wrote a poem about the Statue of Liberty. You can reed it on the base of the statue. part of it says, "Give me your tired, your poor. . . I lift my lamp beside the golden door! The lamp that the statue lifts is a torch the golden door is the united states.

WATCH FOR

- names of people and places
- quotes

**WEDNESDAY**                                        **WEEK 34**

If you go to new york, take a ferry ride out to Liberty Island visit the Statue of Liberty. Read the poem go inside the statue. Look out over new york Harbor. Think of all the peeple who have said, "Thank you! to the Statue of Libertys welcome.

WATCH FOR

- names of people and places

**THURSDAY**                                        **WEEK 34**

Preview the 4 daily lessons to ensure you review or introduce skills that may be unfamiliar to students.

# Helping Sammy

Last July, I was at the ~~beech~~ beach with my family. I was swimming underwater when I heard crying. It was sammy, a clownfish. He was lost. "dont worry, Sammy," I told him. "I'll help you." He looked at me and smiled as a tear rolled down his scales.

**Error Summary**

| | |
|---|---|
| Capitalization | 2 |
| Punctuation: | |
| Apostrophe | 1 |
| Period | 1 |
| Quotation Mark | 2 |
| Spelling | 1 |

**MONDAY**　　　　　　　　　**WEEK 35**

---

Sammy asked between sobs, "What time is it?"

"It's 430," i told him. When ~~she~~ he heard my answer, sammy started ~~cryng~~ crying even harder.

"mom said to be home at 500," he wailed. "you won't be late," I replied. "Let's go!"

**Error Summary**

| | |
|---|---|
| Capitalization | 4 |
| Language Usage | 1 |
| Punctuation: | |
| Apostrophe | 1 |
| Quotation Mark | 3 |
| Other | 2 |
| Spelling | 1 |

**TUESDAY**　　　　　　　　　**WEEK 35**

# Helping Sammy

- dialog

Last July, I was at the beech with my family. I was swimming underwater when I heard crying. It was sammy, a clownfish. He was lost. "dont worry, Sammy, I told him. "I'll help you. He looked at me and smiled as a tear rolled down his scales

**MONDAY**          **WEEK 35**

---

Sammy asked between sobs, What time is it?"

"Its 430," i told him. When she heard my answer, sammy started cryng even harder.

"mom said to be home at 500," he wailed.

you won't be late," I replied. Let's go!"

- dialog
- colons in time

**TUESDAY**          **WEEK 35**

While we were swimming, sammy told me about his home. “there are colorful fish and animals that look like plants. The fish help the animals, and they help us

I said, sammy, my teacher taught me about fish like you. mrs clark said you live in a coral reef!”

| Error Summary | |
|---|---|
| Capitalization | 5 |
| Punctuation: | |
| Period | 2 |
| Quotation Mark | 2 |

WEDNESDAY WEEK 35

We kept swimming. sammy soon saw his family. His mom said, Youre right on time, sammy. Its 500. Would ~~you're~~ your friend like to stay for dinner?”

no, thanks,” I said. Mrs clark had also told me about the bits of shrimp that clownfish eat for dinner!

| Error Summary | |
|---|---|
| Capitalization | 4 |
| Punctuation: | |
| Apostrophe | 2 |
| Period | 1 |
| Quotation Mark | 2 |
| Other | 1 |
| Spelling | 1 |

THURSDAY WEEK 35

While we were swimming, sammy told me about his home. "there are colorful fish and animals that look like plants. The fish help the animals, and they help us

I said, sammy, my teacher taught me about fish like you. mrs clark said you live in a coral reef!"

- dialog

**WEDNESDAY**                    **WEEK 35**

---

We kept swimming. sammy soon saw his family. His mom said, Youre right on time, sammy. Its 500. Would you're friend like to stay for dinner?"

no, thanks," I said. Mrs clark had also told me about the bits of shrimp that clownfish eat for dinner!

- dialog
- colons in time

**THURSDAY**                    **WEEK 35**

Preview the 4 daily lessons to ensure you review or introduce skills that may be unfamiliar to students.

# Presidents in the Mountain

In 1927, Mr. Gutzon borglum began carving huge faces in a tall mountain. The mountain is Mount Rushmore. It reaches more than 1,200 meters (4,000 ft) in the air. The work took mr. borglum many years. He carved the faces of four of americas presidents.

**Error Summary**

| | |
|---|---|
| Capitalization | 4 |
| Punctuation: | |
|   Apostrophe | 1 |
|   Period | 2 |

**MONDAY**       **WEEK 36**

mount Rushmore is in South dakota. It is made of hard rock called "granite" Mr. borglum carved the faces of President washington, president jefferson, President roosevelt, and president lincoln in the granite. There huge faces are 18 meters (60 ft) tall.

Their

**Error Summary**

| | |
|---|---|
| Capitalization | 9 |
| Punctuation: | |
|   Period | 3 |
| Spelling | 1 |

**TUESDAY**       **WEEK 36**

Name _____

# Presidents in the Mountain

WATCH FOR

• names of people
  and places

• abbreviations

In 1927, Mr. Gutzon borglum began carving huge faces in a tall mountain. The mountain is Mount Rushmore. It reaches more than 1,200 meters (4,000 f.t) in the air. The work took mr borglum many years. He carved the faces of four of americas presidents.

**MONDAY**                                           **WEEK 36**

mount Rushmore is in South dakota. It is made of hard rock called "granite" Mr borglum carved the faces of President washington, president jefferson, President roosevelt, and president lincoln in the granite. There huge faces are 18 meters (60 ft) tall.

WATCH FOR

• names of people
  and places

• abbreviations

**TUESDAY**                                          **WEEK 36**

When you visit Mount Rushmore, walk along the Avenue of the Flags. See the ~~flaggs~~ flags for our 50 states. Feel the wind. Look way up at the carvings. Walk the Presidential Trail for 0.8 kilometers (1/2 mi). See a great view of mr. borglums work at the end of the trail.

**Error Summary**

| | |
|---|---|
| Capitalization | 2 |
| Punctuation: | |
|    Apostrophe | 1 |
|    Period | 4 |
| Spelling | 1 |

**WEDNESDAY**                    **WEEK 36**

you will learn about america's past at Mount Rushmore. You will also learn about South dakotas plants and animals. you will see pine and spruce trees. You might ~~sea~~ see a bald eagle. It is a symbol of america. you may even see a mountain goat on the mountain.

**Error Summary**

| | |
|---|---|
| Capitalization | 6 |
| Punctuation: | |
|    Apostrophe | 1 |
|    Period | 1 |
| Spelling | 1 |

**THURSDAY**                    **WEEK 36**

Name _____

When you visit Mount Rushmore, walk along the Avenue of the Flags. See the flaggs for our 50 states. Feel the wind Look way up at the carvings. Walk the Presidential Trail for 0.8 kilometers (1/2 .mi). See a great view of mr borglums work at the end of the trail.

WATCH FOR

• abbreviations
• names of people

| WEDNESDAY | WEEK 36 |

you will learn about america's past at Mount Rushmore. You will also learn about South dakotas plants and animals. you will see pine and spruce trees. You might sea a bald eagle. It is a symbol of america you may even see a mountain goat on the mountain.

WATCH FOR

• names of places

| THURSDAY | WEEK 36 |

Write a paragraph about Jane Goodall and her work. Tell when she first became interested in learning about animals. Explain how she learned about chimps. Be sure to start each sentence with a capital letter and end it with a punctuation mark. Use one of these topic sentences to begin your paragraph, or write your own:

- Jane Goodall has spent most of her life watching animals.

- The work of Jane Goodall has helped scientists learn about the way animals act.

Write a paragraph that tells about where you live. Give the name of your town or city. Also give the name of your state, country, and continent. Don't forget to use a capital letter for the names of places. Use one of these topic sentences, or write your own:

- There are many different ways to tell about where you live.

- I live in a town, a state, a country, and on a continent.

Write a paragraph about exercise. Give examples of ways you can exercise. Also tell what happens to your body when you exercise. Be sure to start all sentences with a capital letter and end them with a period, question mark, or exclamation point. You may use one of these topic sentences to get started:

- Exercise is good for your heart.

- Many exercises make your heart stronger.

Have you ever made or built something? Write a paragraph that tells about something you have made or would like to make. Be sure to use a capital **I** when telling about yourself. When you write a contraction, use an apostrophe (') in the correct place.

Write a paragraph that tells about castles. Tell who lived in a castle and what their life was like. Be sure to begin each sentence with a capital letter and to form plurals correctly. Use one of these topic sentences, or write your own:

- Castles were built to help the people inside stay safe.

- Life in a castle was not as great as you might think.

Write a paragraph about snow. Tell about how snowflakes are formed and what happens when they fall. Remember to capitalize the names of places and months. You might begin your paragraph with one of these topic sentences, or write your own:

- Snowflakes form in the clouds.

- Some places get a lot of snow, while other places get no snow at all.

Write a paragraph that tells about beavers. What makes beavers different from most mammals? Tell about what beavers do and how their bodies help them. Remember to use commas and periods correctly. Start with one of these topic sentences, or write one of your own:

- Beavers have special bodies that help them work.

- Beavers work together to build their homes.

- Beavers are mammals that spend most of the time in the water.

**FRIDAY – WEEK 7**                              **Science Article: Beavers at Work**

Write a paragraph that tells the next part of this story. You could tell about something that happened that night after Jamal and his parents went back to bed. Or, you could tell about what happened the next time the raccoon came back. Use quotation marks around words spoken by people in the story. Also, be sure your sentences begin with a capital letter and tell a complete thought.

**FRIDAY – WEEK 8**                              **Realistic Fiction: Noises in the Night**

What do you think will happen next in the story? Write another paragraph that tells what happens next. Include some words that are spoken to Max. Remember to use quotation marks and commas correctly when someone speaks.

**FRIDAY – WEEK 9**                                        **Description: My Dog Max**

           EMC 2725 • Daily Paragraph Editing, Grade 2 • ©2004 by Evan-Moor Corp.

Write a letter that Sarah and Sid might have sent to their Uncle Wilbur after opening the thank-you present. Remember to use commas in the salutation and closing of the letter. Use your imagination about what was in the box from Uncle Wilbur.

Write a letter to a real or imaginary pen pal or friend who lives in another town, state, or country. Tell the person about something that is happening at your school or at home. Ask your pen pal or friend about what is happening in his or her life. Be sure to use commas after the salutation and closing of your letter.

Write about a book you have read. Be sure to underline the title of the book. If it's a book of poems, be sure to put the titles of poems inside quotation marks. Don't forget to use capital letters for words in titles. Be sure you say what you liked about the book.

Think about your favorite holiday. Write a paragraph that tells about it. Tell where you go and what you do. Remember to use a capital letter for the first letter of someone's name and for the first letter in the name of a holiday. Include one sentence in your paragraph that gives a time. Be sure to use a colon between the hour and the minutes.

Do you think you would like to read <u>Holidays in America</u>? Write a paragraph that tells about the book. Remember to use capital letters for the title of the book, the names of the holidays, and the months of the year. You might want to use one of these topic sentences:

- <u>Holidays in America</u> has lots of facts about holidays.

- There is a great book to help you learn more about holidays.

Write another paragraph about Morris, Jake, and the sticker seeds. Include some words that are spoken when the boys check on the seeds a few weeks later. Be sure to use quotation marks and commas.

Write a paragraph about magnets. Tell what they can do and what they look like. Describe their special force. If you give the name of a book about magnets, be sure to underline the title. You may choose to use one of the following topic sentences, or write one of your own:

- Magnets have a force that you cannot see.

- Books can give you ideas for learning about magnets.

- Magnets have different shapes, sizes, and strengths.

Write a paragraph that tells about George Washington's special barn. Tell what the barn looked liked and how it made it easier to get the kernels off the wheat. Remember to begin each sentence with a capital letter. Be sure each sentence is a complete thought. You may choose to use one of these topic sentences, or write one of your own:

- George Washington was a smart farmer.

- George Washington found a way to make farm work easier.

Have you ever made a gift for someone? Write a paragraph that tells how to make the gift. Remember to use a capital letter for the names of holidays. Be sure to use periods correctly when you write inches (in.) or feet (ft.) the short way.

Write another diary entry from Tim. Tell what happens when his sister Emma comes home. Be sure to use a capital letter for the day and the month of the entry. Use a comma correctly in the date.

Write a paragraph about Benjamin Franklin. Tell about the things he made. Be sure that his name begins with a capital letter. Use periods and question marks correctly. Start with one of these topic sentences, or write one of your own:

- Benjamin Franklin looked for answers to many questions.

- Benjamin Franklin made things that helped many people.

- Benjamin Franklin had lots of good ideas.

Wind learned a lesson from his contest with Sun. Write a paragraph that tells about the Sun and Wind's contest. Tell about the lesson Wind learned. Remember to put a period at the end of a complete thought and to begin each new sentence with a capital letter.

What kind of food do you like to prepare? Write directions for fixing a simple food like cinnamon toast, hot chocolate, or an ice-cream sundae. Remember to use periods at the end of shortened words like **c.** for "cup." Be sure to use commas in a list, too.

Write another paragraph about Danny and Mr. Big. You might tell about their trip home or about another adventure. Be sure to capitalize abbreviations and use periods at the end of them, too.

Write a paragraph that tells about the Great Lakes. Tell where they are located and what makes them special. Don't forget to use a capital letter for the names of the lakes. If you wish, use one of these topic sentences to begin your paragraph:

- The five Great Lakes are like no other lakes in the world.

- The five Great Lakes are Lake Superior, Lake Michigan, Lake Huron, Lake Erie, and Lake Ontario.

Write another paragraph that tells about the next time Tommy uses the odd radio to travel through time. Will he go into the future or into the past? Write about what happens. Be sure to use a colon if you write the time. Use a comma between the day and the year if you write a date.

Write another diary entry from Sara. You might tell something else about her field trip or about her return trip home. Remember to use a capital letter when you write the day and the month. Put a comma in the correct place when you write the date.

Write another part of the interview with Michelle Lee. First, write another question that the writer from <u>Kids' History</u> asks Ms. Lee. Then write the answer that Ms. Lee gives. You might ask who her favorite president is, and why, or about how long it took her to write her new book. If you include the title of the book or magazine, be sure to underline and to use capital letters.

Imagine you are the child that took this trip. Write another paragraph to tell about one of your experiences. You might write about being sick on the wagon train. Include a sentence that mentions your hometown or your new home. Remember to use a capital letter to write the names of places, and to put a comma between the name of a city and a state.

Write a paragraph that tells about the Hubble Space Telescope. Tell where it is and what it does. Remember to use capital letters and periods correctly. You may choose to use one of these topic sentences, or write your own:

- The Hubble Space Telescope helps us learn about things in space.

- Like the moon, the Hubble Space Telescope circles Earth.

Write a paragraph that tells about the properties of objects. Tell how you can describe an object. Tell which tools you can use to learn about each property. Be sure to use periods when you use a short word for a measurement (in., lb., or oz.). Use one of these topic sentences to begin your paragraph, or write your own:

- You can use tools to learn about the size and weight of objects.

- One way to learn more about something is to find its size and weight.

Write a paragraph about the moon. Tell about its light and about the changes in the way it looks. Be sure to capitalize the word **Earth**. Capitalize the names of months and books if you include any. Use a period to end sentences. Start with one of these topic sentences, or write one of your own:

- The amount of sunlight we see on the moon makes it look like the moon changes its shape.

- The moon circles Earth about once every month.

Write a paragraph that tells about Niagara Falls. Remember to use a capital letter for the names of places. Use a period correctly when you write the short form of measurement words, like **ft.** and **yd.** Start your paragraph with one of these topic sentences, or write your own:

- Niagara Falls is in both the United States and Canada.

- Horseshoe Falls and American Falls are both part of Niagara Falls.

What do you think might happen the next time City Mouse visits his cousin in the country? Write a paragraph that tells about this visit. Remember to use commas and quotation marks correctly when one of the mice speaks.

Write a paragraph about the Statue of Liberty. Tell what she looks like and why she is in New York Harbor. Remember to capitalize the names of places. Use one of these topic sentences to begin your paragraph, or write your own:

- A statue of a lady welcomes people coming to America.

- A lady stands tall and proud in the waters of New York Harbor.

Imagine you are the child in this story. What might happen to you as you swim back to the beach and your family? Write a paragraph to tell about that new adventure. Remember to use commas and quotation marks when you write words that someone speaks or thinks.

Write a paragraph that tells about Mount Rushmore. Remember to use a capital letter for the names of places and people. Use a period correctly when you write the short form of words (ft.). Use one of the following topic sentences, or write your own:

- Gutzon Borglum carved the heads of four presidents in Mount Rushmore.

- Mount Rushmore honors four American presidents.

# Language Handbook

## Basic Rules for Writing and Editing

=== Contents ===

**Capital Letters** ............................................................. 169

   Sentences ............................................................. 169

   Greetings/Closings in Letters ............................. 169

   Days, Months, Holidays ...................................... 169

   Names, Titles, and Abbreviations ...................... 169

   Nationalities, Languages, Ethnic Groups .......... 170

   Special Places and Things................................... 170

   Titles .................................................................... 171

**Punctuation Marks** ................................................... 172

   End Punctuation ................................................. 172

      Period (in sentences and abbreviations) ......... 172

      Question Mark............................................... 172

      Exclamation Point ......................................... 172

   Comma ................................................................. 173

   Quotation Marks ................................................. 174

   Apostrophe .......................................................... 175

**Plurals** ........................................................................ 176

EMC 2725 • Daily Paragraph Editing • ©2004 by Evan-Moor Corp.

# Capital Letters

A word that starts with a **capital letter** is special in some way.

Always use a **capital letter** to begin:

| | |
|---|---|
| the first word of a sentence: | Today is the first day of school. |
| the first word of a quotation: | She said, "Today is the first day of school." |
| the salutation (greeting) and closing in a letter: | Dear Grandma,<br>Thanks so much for the birthday gift!<br>Love,<br>Sherry |
| the names of days, months, and holidays: | The fourth Thursday in November is Thanksgiving. |
| people's first and last names, their initials, and their titles: | Mrs. Cruz and her son Felix were both seen by Dr. S. C. Lee.<br><br>**Note:** Many titles can be abbreviated. Use these abbreviations only when you also use the person's name:<br><br>**Mr.** a man    **Capt.** a captain<br>**Mrs.** a married woman    **Lt.** a lieutenant<br>**Ms.** a woman    **Pres.** the president of a country or an organization<br>**Dr.** a doctor |
| the word that names yourself - **I**: | My family and **I** enjoy camping together. |

| a word that is used as a name: | I went with **D**ad and **A**unt **T**erry to visit **G**randma.<br><br>**Be Careful!** Do not use a capital letter at the beginning of a word when it is not used as someone's name:<br><br>I went with my **d**ad and my **a**unt to visit my **g**randma.<br><br>**Hint:** If you can replace the word with a name, it needs a capital letter:<br><br>I went with <u>**D**ad</u>. ⟶ I went with <u>**J**oe</u>. |
|---|---|
| the names of nationalities and languages: | **M**exican, **C**uban, and **N**icaraguan people all speak **S**panish. |
| the names of racial, ethnic, or cultural groups: | There were **A**sian, **N**ative **A**merican, and **A**frican dancers at the festival. |

| to begin the names of these special places and things: | |
|---|---|
| • street names: | **P**alm **A**venue, **C**ypress **S**treet, **P**ine **B**oulevard |
| • cities, states, and countries: | **L**os **A**ngeles, **C**alifornia, **U**nited **S**tates of **A**merica, **P**aris, **F**rance |
| • continents: | **A**sia, **E**urope, **S**outh **A**merica |
| • landforms and bodies of water: | **G**reat **P**lains, **S**an **F**rancisco **B**ay, **G**reat **S**alt **L**ake |
| • buildings, monuments, and public places: | the **W**hite **H**ouse, the **S**tatue of **L**iberty, **Y**ellowstone **N**ational **P**ark |

EMC 2725 • Daily Paragraph Editing • ©2004 by Evan-Moor Corp.

| titles of books, stories, poems, and magazines: | The story "The Friendly Fruit Bat" appeared in <u>Ranger Rick</u> magazine and in a science book called <u>Flying Mammals</u>.<br><br>**Be Careful!** Do not use a capital letter at the beginning of a small word in a title, such as **a**, **an**, **at**, **for**, **in**, and **the**, unless it is the first word in the title.<br><br>**Note:** When you write a title, remember . . .<br>Some titles are underlined:<br>   **Book Titles:** <u>Frog and Toad</u><br>   **Magazine Titles:** <u>Ranger Rick</u><br>   **TV Shows:** <u>Sesame Street</u><br><br>Some titles go inside quotation marks:<br>   **Story Titles:** "The Fox and the Crow"<br>   **Poem Titles:** "My Shadow"<br>   **Song Titles:** "Twinkle, Twinkle, Little Star" |

# Punctuation Marks

**Punctuation** gives information that helps you understand a sentence.

## End Punctuation

Every sentence must end with one of these three punctuation marks:  **. ! ?**

A **period** (.) shows that a sentence is:

| | |
|---|---|
| giving information: | I love to read short stories. |
| giving a mild command: | Choose a short story to read aloud.<br><br>**Note:** A period is also used in:<br><br>• abbreviations of months and days:<br>Jan. (January), Feb. (February),<br>Mon. (Monday), Tue. (Tuesday), etc.<br><br>• abbreviations of measurements:<br>ft. (foot/feet), in. (inch/inches),<br>lb./lbs. (pound/pounds), oz. (ounce/ounces)<br><br>• time:<br>8:00 a.m., 4:30 p.m., etc. |

A **question mark** (?) shows that a sentence is:

| | |
|---|---|
| asking a question: | Did you choose a story to read? |

An **exclamation point** (!) shows that a sentence is:

| | |
|---|---|
| expressing strong feelings: | Wow! That story is really long! |

EMC 2725 • Daily Paragraph Editing • ©2004 by Evan-Moor Corp.

## Comma

A **comma** (**,**) can help you know how to read things. Commas are often used in sentences. Sometimes commas are used with words or phrases.

Some commas are used to keep things separate. Use a **comma** to separate:

| | |
|---|---|
| the name of a city from the name of a state: | El Paso, Texas |
| the name of a city from the name of a country: | London, England |
| the date from the year: | October 12, 2004 |
| the salutation (greeting) from the body of a letter: | Dear Ms. Silver, |
| the closing in a letter from the signature: | Yours truly, |

Some commas help you know where to pause when you read a sentence.
Use a **comma** to show a pause:

| | |
|---|---|
| between three or more items in a list or series: | Nico won't eat beets, spinach, or shrimp. |

## Quotation Marks

Use **quotation marks** (" "):

| | |
|---|---|
| before and after words that are spoken by someone: | "This was the best birthday party ever!" Maya said. |
| | **Note:** Punctuation that follows the speaker's words goes inside the quotation marks: |
| | "May I have a piñata at my birthday party?" Martin asked. |
| | Mr. Flores replied, "You bet!" |
| | **Be Careful!** When the words that tell who is speaking come before the quotation, put the comma outside the quotation marks. When the words that tell who is speaking come after the quotation, put the comma inside the quotation marks: |
| | **Before:** Mrs. Flores asked, "Do you want a chocolate cake, too?" |
| | **After:** "I sure do," said Martin. |

# Apostrophe

An **apostrophe** ( ' ) helps show who owns something. You add an apostrophe after the name of an owner.

| | |
|---|---|
| When there is just one owner, add an apostrophe first and then add an **S**: | cat + 's ⟶ cat's  The cat's dish was empty. |
| When there is more than one owner, add an **S** first and then add an apostrophe: | cats + ' ⟶ cats'  All the cats' cages at the shelter were nice and big.<br><br>**Be Careful!** When the name of more than one owner does not end with an **S**, add an apostrophe first and then add an **S**:<br><br>children + 's ⟶ children's<br><br>The children's cat was in the last cage.<br><br>people + 's ⟶ people's<br><br>Other people's pets were making lots of noise. |
| Use an apostrophe when you put two words together to make one word. This is called a contraction. In a contraction, the apostrophe takes the place of the missing letter or letters: | I + am = I'm<br>you + are = you're<br>he + is = he's<br>it + is = it's<br>we + would = we'd<br>they + will = they'll<br>do + not = don't<br>does + not = doesn't<br>are + not = aren't<br>could + not = couldn't<br>have + not = haven't<br>would + not = wouldn't |

# Plurals

A noun names a person, place, or thing. A **plural noun** names more than one person, place, or thing.

| | |
|---|---|
| Add an **s** to make most nouns plural: | girl ⟶ girl + s ⟶ girl**s**<br>river ⟶ river + s ⟶ river**s** |
| If the noun ends in **ch**, **s**, **sh**, or **x**, add **es**: | lunch ⟶ lunch + es ⟶ lunch**es**<br>dress ⟶ dress + es ⟶ dress**es**<br>brush ⟶ brush + es ⟶ brush**es**<br>fox ⟶ fox + es ⟶ fox**es** |
| If the noun ends in **y**, change the y to **i** and add **es**: | fly ⟶ fli + es ⟶ fli**es**<br>story ⟶ stori + es ⟶ stori**es**<br><br>**Note:** If the noun ends in a vowel plus **y**, just add **s**:<br><br>    bay ⟶ bay + s ⟶ bay**s**<br>    key ⟶ key + s ⟶ key**s**<br>    boy ⟶ boy + s ⟶ boy**s**<br><br>**Be Careful!** Some plural nouns do not have an **s** at all:<br><br>    child ⟶ **children**        foot ⟶ **feet**<br>    man ⟶ **men**            tooth ⟶ **teeth**<br>    woman ⟶ **women**      goose ⟶ **geese** |

EMC 2725 • Daily Paragraph Editing • ©2004 by Evan-Moor Corp.